CS-42 GENERAL APTITUDE AND ABILITIES SERIES

*This is your
PASSBOOK for...*

How to Prepare for a Civil Service Examination (TEXT)

*Test Preparation Study Guide
Questions & Answers*

NATIONAL LEARNING CORPORATION®

COPYRIGHT NOTICE

This book is SOLELY intended for, is sold ONLY to, and its use is RESTRICTED to individual, bona fide applicants or candidates who qualify by virtue of having seriously filed applications for appropriate license, certificate, professional and/or promotional advancement, higher school matriculation, scholarship, or other legitimate requirements of education and/or governmental authorities.

This book is NOT intended for use, class instruction, tutoring, training, duplication, copying, reprinting, excerption, or adaptation, etc., by:

1) Other publishers
2) Proprietors and/or Instructors of "Coaching" and/or Preparatory Courses
3) Personnel and/or Training Divisions of commercial, industrial, and governmental organizations
4) Schools, colleges, or universities and/or their departments and staffs, including teachers and other personnel
5) Testing Agencies or Bureaus
6) Study groups which seek by the purchase of a single volume to copy and/or duplicate and/or adapt this material for use by the group as a whole without having purchased individual volumes for each of the members of the group
7) Et al.

Such persons would be in violation of appropriate Federal and State statutes.

PROVISION OF LICENSING AGREEMENTS – Recognized educational, commercial, industrial, and governmental institutions and organizations, and others legitimately engaged in educational pursuits, including training, testing, and measurement activities, may address request for a licensing agreement to the copyright owners, who will determine whether, and under what conditions, including fees and charges, the materials in this book may be used them. In other words, a licensing facility exists for the legitimate use of the material in this book on other than an individual basis. However, it is asseverated and affirmed here that the material in this book CANNOT be used without the receipt of the express permission of such a licensing agreement from the Publishers. Inquiries re licensing should be addressed to the company, attention rights and permissions department.

All rights reserved, including the right of reproduction in whole or in part, in any form or by any means, electronic or mechanical, including photocopying, recording, or by any information storage and retrieval system, without permission in writing from the Publisher.

Copyright © 2024 by
National Learning Corporation

212 Michael Drive, Syosset, NY 11791
(516) 921-8888 • www.passbooks.com
E-mail: info@passbooks.com

PUBLISHED IN THE UNITED STATES OF AMERICA

PASSBOOK® SERIES

THE *PASSBOOK® SERIES* has been created to prepare applicants and candidates for the ultimate academic battlefield – the examination room.

At some time in our lives, each and every one of us may be required to take an examination – for validation, matriculation, admission, qualification, registration, certification, or licensure.

Based on the assumption that every applicant or candidate has met the basic formal educational standards, has taken the required number of courses, and read the necessary texts, the *PASSBOOK® SERIES* furnishes the one special preparation which may assure passing with confidence, instead of failing with insecurity. Examination questions – together with answers – are furnished as the basic vehicle for study so that the mysteries of the examination and its compounding difficulties may be eliminated or diminished by a sure method.

This book is meant to help you pass your examination provided that you qualify and are serious in your objective.

The entire field is reviewed through the huge store of content information which is succinctly presented through a provocative and challenging approach – the question-and-answer method.

A climate of success is established by furnishing the correct answers at the end of each test.

You soon learn to recognize types of questions, forms of questions, and patterns of questioning. You may even begin to anticipate expected outcomes.

You perceive that many questions are repeated or adapted so that you can gain acute insights, which may enable you to score many sure points.

You learn how to confront new questions, or types of questions, and to attack them confidently and work out the correct answers.

You note objectives and emphases, and recognize pitfalls and dangers, so that you may make positive educational adjustments.

Moreover, you are kept fully informed in relation to new concepts, methods, practices, and directions in the field.

You discover that you are actually taking the examination all the time: you are preparing for the examination by "taking" an examination, not by reading extraneous and/or supererogatory textbooks.

In short, this PASSBOOK®, used directedly, should be an important factor in helping you to pass your test.

HOW TO PREPARE FOR A CIVIL SERVICE EXAMINATION

This pamphlet will introduce you to civil service examinations. You will get some advice on preparing for written tests. You will also see sample written test questions.

First, we would like to give you some background. WHY A TEST?

The State Constitution says their public employees must be hired for jobs on the basis of their merit and fitness. The constitution also says the examinations have to be used to measure merit and fitness for most jobs.

In practical terms, *merit and fitness* means finding people who are best suited to a particular job. The idea is to hire people who will be able to do the job well. In fact, the State is no different from private companies. Any employer wants workers who can do a good job.

There are several ways to find good workers. When private companies hire, they ask people what kind of work they have done in the past and how they would do the company's job. They also look at resumes and school records. Sometimes they give tests.

Through civil service examinations, the State does many of things in a structured way that private companies do when they hire.

Written and oral tests are designed to find out how people would do the State's job. Evaluation of training and experience is a detailed look at applications and resumes. Performance tests are tasks that measure certain skills, like typing or entering data at computer terminals.

All examinations are based on the kind of job to be filled. The major difference between examinations and other ways of hiring is that examinations all use some kind of formal rating scale or system that is as fair and objective as possible. Each candidate for an examination answers the same questions or does the same task. In any test, all candidates receive a score (rating) based on the same factors. This helps make sure that everyone has a fair and equal chance to get a job and it helps the State find the people best suited to the available jobs. This is the why behind examinations.

HOW TO TAKE A TEST

You have studied long, hard and conscientiously.

With your official admission card in hand, and your heart pounding, you have been admitted to the examination room.

You note that there are several hundred other applicants in the examination room waiting to take the same test.

They all appear to be equally well prepared.

You know that nothing but your best effort will suffice. The "moment of truth" is at hand: you now have to demonstrate objectively, in writing, your knowledge of content and your understanding of subject matter.

You are fighting the most important battle of your life—to pass and/or score high on an examination which will determine your career and provide the economic basis for your livelihood.

What extra, special things should you know and should you do in taking the examination?

I. YOU MUST PASS AN EXAMINATION

A. WHAT EVERY CANDIDATE SHOULD KNOW
Examination applicants often ask us for help in preparing for the written test. What can I study in advance? What kinds of questions will be asked? How will the test be given? How will the papers be graded?

B. HOW ARE EXAMS DEVELOPED?
Examinations are carefully written by trained technicians who are specialists in the field known as "psychological measurement," in consultation with recognized authorities in the field of work that the test will cover. These experts recommend the subject matter areas or skills to be tested; only those knowledges or skills important to your success on the job are included. The most reliable books and source materials available are used as references. Together, the experts and technicians judge the difficulty level of the questions.
Test technicians know how to phrase questions so that the problem is clearly stated. Their ethics do not permit "trick" or "catch" questions. Questions may have been tried out on sample groups, or subjected to statistical analysis, to determine their usefulness.
Written tests are often used in combination with performance tests, ratings of training and experience, and oral interviews. All of these measures combine to form the best-known means of finding the right person for the right job.

II. HOW TO PASS THE WRITTEN TEST

A. BASIC STEPS

1) Study the announcement

How, then, can you know what subjects to study? Our best answer is: "Learn as much as possible about the class of positions for which you've applied." The exam will test the knowledge, skills and abilities needed to do the work.

Your most valuable source of information about the position you want is the official exam announcement. This announcement lists the training and experience qualifications. Check these standards and apply only if you come reasonably close to meeting them. Many jurisdictions preview the written test in the exam announcement by including a section called "Knowledge and Abilities Required," "Scope of the Examination," or some similar heading. Here you will find out specifically what fields will be tested.

2) Choose appropriate study materials

If the position for which you are applying is technical or advanced, you will read more advanced, specialized material. If you are already familiar with the basic principles of your field, elementary textbooks would waste your time. Concentrate on advanced textbooks and technical periodicals. Think through the concepts and review difficult problems in your field.

These are all general sources. You can get more ideas on your own initiative, following these leads. For example, training manuals and publications of the government agency which employs workers in your field can be useful, particularly for technical and professional positions. A letter or visit to the government department involved may result in more specific study suggestions, and certainly will provide you with a more definite idea of the exact nature of the position you are seeking.

3) Study this book!

III. KINDS OF TESTS

Tests are used for purposes other than measuring knowledge and ability to perform specified duties. For some positions, it is equally important to test ability to make adjustments to new situations or to profit from training. In others, basic mental abilities not dependent on information are essential. Questions which test these things may not appear as pertinent to the duties of the position as those which test for knowledge and information. Yet they are often highly important parts of a fair examination. For very general questions, it is almost impossible to help you direct your study efforts. What we can do is to point out some of the more common of these general abilities needed in public service positions and describe some typical questions.

1) General information

Broad, general information has been found useful for predicting job success in some kinds of work. This is tested in a variety of ways, from vocabulary lists to questions about current events. Basic background in some field of work, such as sociology or economics, may be sampled in a group of questions. Often these are principles which have become familiar to most persons through exposure rather than through formal training. It is difficult to advise you how to study for these questions; being alert to the world around you is our best suggestion.

2) Verbal ability

An example of an ability needed in many positions is verbal or language ability. Verbal ability is, in brief, the ability to use and understand words. Vocabulary and grammar tests are typical measures of this ability. Reading comprehension or paragraph interpretation questions are common in many kinds of civil service tests. You are given a paragraph of written material and asked to find its central meaning.

IV. KINDS OF QUESTIONS

1. Multiple-choice Questions

Most popular of the short-answer questions is the "multiple choice" or "best answer" question. It can be used, for example, to test for factual knowledge, ability to solve problems or judgment in meeting situations found at work.

A multiple-choice question is normally one of three types:
- It can begin with an incomplete statement followed by several possible endings. You are to find the one ending which best completes the statement, although some of the others may not be entirely wrong.
- It can also be a complete statement in the form of a question which is answered by choosing one of the statements listed.
- It can be in the form of a problem – again you select the best answer.

Here is an example of a multiple-choice question with a discussion which should give you some clues as to the method for choosing the right answer:

When an employee has a complaint about his assignment, the action which will best help him overcome his difficulty is to
    A. discuss his difficulty with his coworkers
    B. take the problem to the head of the organization
    C. take the problem to the person who gave him the assignment
    D. say nothing to anyone about his complaint

In answering this question, you should study each of the choices to find which is best. Consider choice "A" – Certainly an employee may discuss his complaint with fellow employees, but no change or improvement can result, and the complaint remains unresolved. Choice "B" is a poor choice since the head of the organization probably does not know what assignment you have been given, and taking your problem to him is known as "going over the head" of the supervisor. The supervisor, or person who made the assignment, is the person who can clarify it or correct any injustice. Choice "C" is, therefore, correct. To say nothing, as in choice "D," is unwise. Supervisors have and interest in knowing the problems employees are facing, and the employee is seeking a solution to his problem.

2. True/False

3. Matching Questions

Matching an answer from a column of choices within another column.

V. RECORDING YOUR ANSWERS

Computer terminals are used more and more today for many different kinds of exams.

For an examination with very few applicants, you may be told to record your answers in the test booklet itself. Separate answer sheets are much more common. If this separate answer sheet is to be scored by machine – and this is often the case – it is highly important that you mark your answers correctly in order to get credit.

VI. BEFORE THE TEST

YOUR PHYSICAL CONDITION IS IMPORTANT

If you are not well, you can't do your best work on tests. If you are half asleep, you can't do your best either. Here are some tips:

1) Get about the same amount of sleep you usually get. Don't stay up all night before the test, either partying or worrying—DON'T DO IT!
2) If you wear glasses, be sure to wear them when you go to take the test. This goes for hearing aids, too.
3) If you have any physical problems that may keep you from doing your best, be sure to tell the person giving the test. If you are sick or in poor health, you relay cannot do your best on any test. You can always come back and take the test some other time.

Common sense will help you find procedures to follow to get ready for an examination. Too many of us, however, overlook these sensible measures. Indeed, nervousness and fatigue have been found to be the most serious reasons why applicants fail to do their best on civil service tests. Here is a list of reminders:

- Begin your preparation early – Don't wait until the last minute to go scurrying around for books and materials or to find out what the position is all about.
- Prepare continuously – An hour a night for a week is better than an all-night cram session. This has been definitely established. What is more, a night a week for a month will return better dividends than crowding your study into a shorter period of time.
- Locate the place of the exam – You have been sent a notice telling you when and where to report for the examination. If the location is in a different town or otherwise unfamiliar to you, it would be well to inquire the best route and learn something about the building.
- Relax the night before the test – Allow your mind to rest. Do not study at all that night. Plan some mild recreation or diversion; then go to bed early and get a good night's sleep.
- Get up early enough to make a leisurely trip to the place for the test – This way unforeseen events, traffic snarls, unfamiliar buildings, etc. will not upset you.
- Dress comfortably – A written test is not a fashion show. You will be known by number and not by name, so wear something comfortable.
- Leave excess paraphernalia at home – Shopping bags and odd bundles will get in your way. You need bring only the items mentioned in the official notice you received; usually everything you need is provided. Do not bring reference books to the exam. They will only confuse those last minutes and be taken away from you when in the test room.

- Arrive somewhat ahead of time – If because of transportation schedules you must get there very early, bring a newspaper or magazine to take your mind off yourself while waiting.
- Locate the examination room – When you have found the proper room, you will be directed to the seat or part of the room where you will sit. Sometimes you are given a sheet of instructions to read while you are waiting. Do not fill out any forms until you are told to do so; just read them and be prepared.
- Relax and prepare to listen to the instructions
- If you have any physical problem that may keep you from doing your best, be sure to tell the test administrator. If you are sick or in poor health, you really cannot do your best on the exam. You can come back and take the test some other time.

VII. AT THE TEST

The day of the test is here and you have the test booklet in your hand. The temptation to get going is very strong. Caution! There is more to success than knowing the right answers. You must know how to identify your papers and understand variations in the type of short-answer question used in this particular examination. Follow these suggestions for maximum results from your efforts:

1) Cooperate with the monitor

The test administrator has a duty to create a situation in which you can be as much at ease as possible. He will give instructions, tell you when to begin, check to see that you are marking your answer sheet correctly, and so on. He is not there to guard you, although he will see that your competitors do not take unfair advantage. He wants to help you do your best.

2) Listen to all instructions

Don't jump the gun! Wait until you understand all directions. In most civil service tests you get more time than you need to answer the questions. So don't be in a hurry. Read each word of instructions until you clearly understand the meaning. Study the examples, listen to all announcements and follow directions. Ask questions if you do not understand what to do.

3) Identify your papers

Civil service exams are usually identified by number only. You will be assigned a number; you must not put your name on your test papers. Be sure to copy your number correctly. Since more than one exam may be given, copy your exact examination title.

4) Plan your time

Unless you are told that a test is a "speed" or "rate of work" test, speed itself is usually not important. Time enough to answer all the questions will be provided, but this does not mean that you have all day. An overall time limit has been set. Divide the total time (in minutes) by the number of questions to determine the approximate time you have for each question.

5) Do not linger over difficult questions

If you come across a difficult question, mark it with a paper clip (useful to have along) and come back to it when you have been through the booklet. One caution if you do this – be sure to skip a number on your answer sheet as well. Check often to be sure that you have not lost your place and that you are marking in the row numbered the same as the question you are answering.

6) Read the questions

Be sure you know what the question asks! Many capable people are unsuccessful because they failed to read the questions correctly.

7) Answer all questions

Unless you have been instructed that a penalty will be deducted for incorrect answers, it is better to guess than to omit a question.

8) Speed tests

It is often better NOT to guess on speed tests. It has been found that on timed tests people are tempted to spend the last few seconds before time is called in marking answers at random – without even reading them – in the hope of picking up a few extra points. To discourage this practice, the instructions may warn you that your score will be "corrected" for guessing. That is, a penalty will be applied. The incorrect answers will be deducted from the correct ones, or some other penalty formula will be used.

9) Review your answers

If you finish before time is called, go back to the questions you guessed or omitted to give them further thought. Review other answers if you have time.

10) Return your test materials

If you are ready to leave before others have finished or time is called, take ALL your materials to the monitor and leave quietly. Never take any test material with you. The monitor can discover whose papers are not complete, and taking a test booklet may be grounds for disqualification.

VIII. EXAMINATION TECHNIQUES

1) Read the general instructions carefully. These are usually printed on the first page of the exam booklet. As a rule, these instructions refer to the timing of the examination; the fact that you should not start work until the signal and must stop work at a signal, etc. If there are any special instructions, such as a choice of questions to be answered, make sure that you note this instruction carefully.

2) When you are ready to start work on the examination, that is as soon as the signal has been given, read the instructions to each question booklet, underline any key words or phrases, such as least, best, outline, describe and the like. In this way you will tend to answer as requested rather than discover on reviewing your paper that you listed without describing, that you selected the worst choice rather than the best choice, etc.

3) If the examination is of the objective or multiple-choice type – that is, each question will also give a series of possible answers: A, B, C or D, and you are called upon to select the best answer and write the letter next to that answer on your answer paper – it is advisable to start answering each question in turn. There may be anywhere from 50 to 100 such questions in the three or four hours allotted and you can see how much time would be taken if you read through all the questions before beginning to answer any. Furthermore, if you

come across a question or group of questions which you know would be difficult to answer, it would undoubtedly affect your handling of all the other questions.

4) If the examination is of the essay type and contains but a few questions, it is a moot point as to whether you should read all the questions before starting to answer any one. Of course, if you are given a choice – say five out of seven and the like – then it is essential to read all the questions so you can eliminate the two that are most difficult. If, however, you are asked to answer all the questions, there may be danger in trying to answer the easiest one first because you may find that you will spend too much time on it. The best technique is to answer the first question, then proceed to the second, etc.

5) Time your answers. Before the exam begins, write down the time it started, then add the time allowed for the examination and write down the time it must be completed, then divide the time available somewhat as follows:
   - If 3-1/2 hours are allowed, that would be 210 minutes. If you have 80 objective-type questions, that would be an average of 2-1/2 minutes per question. Allow yourself no more than 2 minutes per question, or a total of 160 minutes, which will permit about 50 minutes to review.
   - If for the time allotment of 210 minutes there are 7 essay questions to answer, that would average about 30 minutes a question. Give yourself only 25 minutes per question so that you have about 35 minutes to review.

6) The most important instruction is to read each question and make sure you know what is wanted. The second most important instruction is to time yourself properly so that you answer every question. The third most important instruction is to answer every question. Guess if you have to but include something for each question. Remember that you will receive no credit for a blank and will probably receive some credit if you write something in answer to an essay question. If you guess a letter – say "B" for a multiple-choice question – you may have guessed right. If you leave a blank as an answer to a multiple-choice question, the examiners may respect your feelings but it will not add a point to your score. Some exams may penalize you for wrong answers, so in such cases only, you may not want to guess unless you have some basis for your answer.

7) Suggestions
   a. Objective-type questions
      1. Examine the question booklet for proper sequence of pages and questions
      2. Read all instructions carefully
      3. Skip any question which seems too difficult; return to it after all other questions have been answered
      4. Apportion your time properly; do not spend too much time on any single question or group of questions
      5. Note and underline key words – all, most, fewest, least, best, worst, same, opposite, etc.
      6. Pay particular attention to negatives
      7. Note unusual option, e.g., unduly long, short, complex, different or similar in content to the body of the question
      8. Observe the use of "hedging" words – probably, may, most likely, etc.

9. Make sure that your answer is put next to the same number as the question
10. Do not second-guess unless you have good reason to believe the second answer is definitely more correct
11. Cross out original answer if you decide another answer is more accurate; do not erase until you are ready to hand your paper in
12. Answer all questions; guess unless instructed otherwise
13. Leave time for review

b. Essay questions
1. Read each question carefully
2. Determine exactly what is wanted. Underline key words or phrases.
3. Decide on outline or paragraph answer
4. Include many different points and elements unless asked to develop any one or two points or elements
5. Show impartiality by giving pros and cons unless directed to select one side only
6. Make and write down any assumptions you find necessary to answer the questions
7. Watch your English, grammar, punctuation and choice of words
8. Time your answers; don't crowd material

8) Answering the essay question

Most essay questions can be answered by framing the specific response around several key words or ideas. Here are a few such key words or ideas:

M's: manpower, materials, methods, money, management
P's: purpose, program, policy, plan, procedure, practice, problems, pitfalls, personnel, public relations

a. Six basic steps in handling problems:
1. Preliminary plan and background development
2. Collect information, data and facts
3. Analyze and interpret information, data and facts
4. Analyze and develop solutions as well as make recommendations
5. Prepare report and sell recommendations
6. Install recommendations and follow up effectiveness

b. Pitfalls to avoid
1. Taking things for granted – A statement of the situation does not necessarily imply that each of the elements is necessarily true; for example, a complaint may be invalid and biased so that all that can be taken for granted is that a complaint has been registered
2. Considering only one side of a situation – Wherever possible, indicate several alternatives and then point out the reasons you selected the best one
3. Failing to indicate follow up – Whenever your answer indicates action on your part, make certain that you will take proper follow-up action to see how successful your recommendations, procedures or actions turn out to be
4. Taking too long in answering any single question – Remember to time your answers properly

EXAMINATION SECTION

FINDING A JOB

TABLE OF CONTENTS

	Page
INTRODUCTION	1
PLANNING YOUR TIME	2
DETERMINING YOUR JOB SKILLS	3
MATCHING YOUR BACKGROUND AND EXPERIENCE TO JOBS	4
WHERE TO GET JOB INFORMATION	4
COVER LETTERS AND APPLICATIONS	6
PREPARING YOUR RESUME	6
10 TIPS FOR THE EFFECTIVE RESUME	8
COMMON QUESTIONS ABOUT RESUMES	9
INTERVIEWING	10
COMMON QUESTIONS ABOUT INTERVIEWS	11
TESTING	13
AFTER THE INTERVIEW	14
JOB SEARCH CHECKLIST	15
MOST COMMON JOB-HUNTING MISTAKES	16
COMMON QUESTIONS ABOUT THE FOLLOW-UP	18
AFTER YOU ARE HIRED	18

FINDING A JOB

INTRODUCTION

You need a job. Somewhere, an employer has the job you want. How do you get that job? By marketing your job talents. By showing employers you have the skills they need.

Do you have job talents? Yes! Homemakers, disabled individuals, veterans, students just out of school, people already working—all have skills and experience for many good jobs.

What you need to know is how to market your talents effectively to find the right job. This guide will help you to:

- Evaluate your interests and skills
- Find job information
- Write resumes and application letters
- Prepare and plan for job interviews
- Plan your time
- Take tests

PLANNING YOUR TIME

Now is the best time to start looking for a job. You're as qualified as other applicants, so start now before someone else gets "your" job. You've already made a good start by reading this guide!

What's the most important thing to know about your job search?
<u>Finding work is a full-time job.</u>

In a full-time job, you:
- Have responsibilities (work duties and procedures)
- "Punch a clock" or be at work "on time"
- Work hard all day, 40 hours a week
- Report to a boss, who makes sure you carry out your responsibilities

To find a job, you must:
- Set your own responsibilities (things you must do every day to get a job)
- Wake up early at a set time to start looking for work
- Look hard for a job, all day, 40 hours a week
- Be your own boss (or appoint a friend to be your "boss") to make sure you carry out your job search responsibilities

Tips for Planning an Effective Job Search:

- Make a "To Do List" every day. Outline daily activities to look for a job.
- Apply for jobs early in the day. This will make a good impression and give you time to complete applications, have interviews, take tests, etc.
- Call employers to find out the best times to apply. Some companies take applications only on certain days and times during the week.
- Write down all employers you contact, the date of your contacts, people you talk to, and special notes about your contacts.
- Apply at several companies in the same area when possible. This saves time and money.
- Be prepared. Have a "master application" and resumes, pens, maps and job information with you all the time. Who knows when a "hot lead" will come your way.
- Follow up leads immediately. If you find out about a job late in the day, call right then! Don't wait until the next day.
- Network. Tell everyone you know that you're looking for a job. Stay in touch with friends and contacts. Follow up new leads immediately.
- Read pamphlets and books on how to get a job. The time you spend reading these materials will save you a lot of time in your job search.
- Make automated connections through systems on the Internet, such as America's Job Bank and the Talent Bank.

DETERMINING YOUR JOB SKILLS

Another tip for finding the right job: *Make a list of your background experience.*

If you think you don't have any experience—think again! You may not have specific job experience, but you do have work experience. You have "worked" as a homemaker, a student, a volunteer, in a hobby or some other personal activity. The skills you use for these "jobs" can be applied to other jobs.

A background and experience list may help you to fill out job applications, provide information for job interviews and prepare resumes (if you're applying for professional or office jobs).

Tips for Making a Background and Experience List:

Interests and Aptitudes
- List your hobbies, clubs you belong to, sports you're involved in, church and school activities, and things that interest you. List things you are good at or have special ability for.
- Look at the first item on your list. Think about the skills or talents it takes to do that item. Really think about it! All hobbies, activities, etc. take a lot of skills, knowledge and abilities. For example, playing basketball requires the ability to interact with others (be a "team player") and the ability to lead or direct teammates/coworkers. Homemaking requires the ability to manage budgets, handle multiple tasks and the skills to teach or train others. Fixing cars requires knowledge of electronics and machinery, and the ability to diagnose mechanical problems.

Work History
If you've worked before, list your jobs. Include volunteer, part-time, summer and self-employment. Next, write down work duties for the jobs you listed. Now think about the skills and talents it took to do each work duty. Write them down.

Education
- List the schools you attended, dates, major studies or courses completed. Include military and vocational education and on-the-job training
- List degrees, certificates, awards and honors
- Ask yourself what classes or training you like and why

Physical Condition
- Do you have any disabilities limiting the kind of work you can do? Companies will often make special accommodations to employ disabled persons (in fact, some accommodations are legally required). If you have strong or special physical capabilities, list these too.

Career Goals
- What kind of work do you want to be doing 5 or 10 years from now? What kind of job could you get now to help you reach this goal?

MATCHING YOUR BACKGROUND AND EXPERIENCE TO JOBS

Look at the abilities (talents) identified on your background and experience list. You have talents that you use every day. Now find out what jobs can use your talents.

Start at your local State Employment Service Office ("Job Service"). This office has free information about many jobs. You may be given an appointment with a career counselor who can help you decide what kind of work is best suited to your abilities and interests.

While you're at Job Service, ask to see the *Guide for Occupational Exploration* and the *Occupational Outlook Handbook* (you can also get these books at most public libraries). These easy-to-read books, published by the Department of Labor, describe work duties for different occupations, skills and abilities needed for different types of jobs, how to enter occupations, where jobs are located, training and qualifications needed, as well as earnings, working conditions and future opportunities.

Match the skills and abilities in your list to the skills and abilities of different jobs. Don't limit yourself. The important thing is not the job title, but the skills and abilities of the job. You may find that your abilities match with an occupation that you have never thought about.

WHERE TO GET JOB INFORMATION

If you know what job skills you have, you are ready to look for a job. You can look for job openings at these sources:

- Networking – Tell everyone you know you're looking for a job. Ask about openings where your friends work.
- Private employers – Contact employers directly to market your job talents. Talk to the person who would supervise you even if there are no jobs currently open.
- State Employment Service Offices provide help on finding jobs and other services, such as career counseling
- America's Job Bank – A nationwide pool of job opportunities which will extend your search to other states and can be viewed in your local Employment Service offices or on the Internet at http://www.ajb.dni.us
- Federal, state and local government personnel offices list a wide range of job opportunities. Check the government listings in your phone book.
- Local public libraries have books on occupations and often post local job announcements. Many state libraries are also providing free access to Internet through PCs.
- Newspaper ads list various job openings
- Local phone book – Look for career counseling centers in your area
- Private employment and temporary agencies offer placement (employer or job hunter may pay a fee)
- Community colleges and trade schools usually offer counseling and job information to students and the general public
- Proprietary schools – Private training centers offer instruction in specific trades (tuition is usually required). Check with your office of state education for credible schools.

- Community organizations such as clubs, associations, women and minority centers, and youth organizations
- Churches frequently operate employment services or provide job search help
- Veterans' placement centers operate through State Employment Service Offices. Veterans' social and help organizations often have job listings for members.
- Union and apprenticeship programs provide job opportunities and information. Contact your state apprenticeship council or relevant labor union directly.
- Government sponsored training programs offer direct placement or short-term training and placement for applicants who qualify. Check the yellow pages under Job Training Programs or Government Services.
- Journals and newsletters for professional or trade associations often advertise job openings in their field. Ask for these at the local library.

Under the Civil Rights Act of 1964, as amended in 1991, all of the sources listed above serve persons of any race, color, religion, sex or national origin. The Age Discrimination in Employment Act of 1967 forbids agencies to discriminate against older workers. Both laws forbid employers to discriminate in hiring.

In addition, the Americans with Disabilities Act under Title I prohibits employment discrimination against "qualified individuals with disabilities." A qualified individual with a disability is: an individual with a disability who meets the skill, experience, education and other job-related requirements of a position held or desired, and who, with or without reasonable accommodation, can perform the essential functions of a job.

MOST COMMONLY USED JOB SEARCH METHODS

Percent of Jobseekers Using this Method	Method	Effectiveness Rate
66.0%	Applied directly to employer	47.7%
50.8	Asked friends about jobs where they work	22.1
41.8	Asked friends about jobs elsewhere	11.9
28.4	Asked relatives about jobs where they work	19.3
27.3	Asked relatives about jobs elsewhere	7.4
45.9	Answered local newspaper ads	23.9
21.0	Private employment agency	24.2
12.5	School placement office	21.4
15.3	Civil Service test	12.5
10.4	Asked teacher or professor	12.1
1.6	Placed ad in local newspaper	12.9
6.0	Union hiring hall	22.2

COVER LETTERS AND APPLICATIONS

A letter of application is used when inquiring about a job or submitting an application form. If you're applying for a job that requires a resume, you should write a cover letter to accompany your resume. The purpose of these cover letters is to:
- Tell how your job talents will benefit the company
- Show why the employer should read your resume or application form
- Ask for a job interview

Tips for Writing Cover Letters
- Write a separate letter for each job application
- Type letters on quality 8 1/2" x 11" paper
- Use proper sentence structure and correct spelling and punctuation
- Convey personal interest and enthusiasm
- Keep your letter short and to the point
- Show that you've done some homework on the company (you know what they do, their interests and problems)
- Try to identify something about you that is unique or of interest to the employer
- Request an interview, and if possible, suggest a date and time
- Include your address and telephone number
- Address each letter to the specific person you want to talk to (the person who would actually supervise you)
- Highlight your job qualifications
- State the position you are seeking and the source of the job opening

PREPARING YOUR RESUME

You want to apply for a job. Do you need a resume? That depends on the kind of job you are applying for:
   * Professional, technical, administrative and managerial jobs, as well as sales, secretarial, clerical and other office jobs require a resume.
   * Skilled jobs (ex. baker, hotel clerk, electrician, drafter, welder, etc.) sometimes require a resume.
   * Unskilled, quick turnover jobs (ex. fast food server, laborers, machine loader, etc.) do not require a resume.

Tips for Good Resumes

You need two types of information to prepare your resume:
1. Self-information – You need to know your job talents, work history, education and career goals. Did you complete your background and experience list? If you did, you have the self-information required to prepare your resume.
1. Job information – Gather specific information on the job you're applying for. Here's what you need:
   - Job duties (to match your skills to the skills needed for the job). Get your job duties from the job announcement. If the announcement or ad is vague, call the employer and ask for a description of job duties.
   - Education and experience required
   - Hours and shifts usually worked

- Pay range (make their top offer the minimum acceptable!)

With the information on yourself and the job you're applying for, you're ready to write your resume.

Two Types of Resumes

Reverse Chronological – lists jobs you've had. Your most recent job is listed first, your job before that is listed second, and so on. Each job has employment dates and job duties.

Functional – describes your skills, abilities and accomplishments that relate to the job you're applying for. Employment history is less detailed than chronological resumes.

What kind of resume should you use? Answer the following questions:
- Have you progressed up a clearly defined career ladder, and you're looking for job advancement?
- Do you have recent job experience at one or more companies?

If you're answer is yes, use a reverse chronological resume.

- Are you a displaced homemaker?
- Are you a veteran and you want to relate your military training to civilian jobs?
- Do you have little or no job experience?
- Do you have gaps in your work history?
- Is the job you're applying for different from your present or recent job?
- Do you want to emphasize your work skills and accomplishments instead of describing your job duties?

If your answer to any of these is yes, use a functional resume.

Tips for Preparing a Functional Resume
- Study the duties for the job you're applying for. Identify two or three general skills that are important to the job.
- Review your background and experience list. Find talents and accomplishments that demonstrate your ability to perform the job skills.
- List your talents and accomplishments under the job skills they relate to
- Use simple, short, active sentences
- Focus attention on strong points

Tips for Preparing a Reverse Chronological Resume
- List your jobs starting with your present or most recent job. Give exact dates for each job.
- Briefly describe the main duties you performed in each job
- Emphasize duties that are important for the job you're applying for
- Use simple, short, active sentences
- Include scholarships and honors and major school subjects if related to your job goal

10 TIPS FOR THE EFFECTIVE RESUME

The following rules apply to all resumes:

1. If possible, use a computer to prepare your resume. There are computer programs that make it easy to produce a professional looking resume. Your local school, library, Employment Service local office or "quick print" shop can help.
2. Do not include irrelevant personal information (age, weight, height, marital status, etc.)
3. Do not include salary and wages
4. Center or justify all headings – Don't use abbreviations
5. Be positive and identify accomplishments
6. Use action verbs
7. Be specific – Use concise sentences, keep it short (one page is best)
8. Make sure your resume "looks good" (neat and readable)
9. Proofread the master copy carefully. Have someone else proofread it also.
10. Inspect photocopies for clarity, smudges and marks

Action Verbs

Action verbs give your resume power and direction. Try to begin all skills statements with an action verb. Here is a sample of action verbs for different types of skills:

Management	Technical	Clerical	Communication
administered	assembled	arranged	arranged
analyzed	built	catalogued	addressed
coordinated	calculated	compiled	authored
developed	designed	generated	drafted
directed	operated	organized	formulated
evaluated	overhauled	processed	
improved	remodeled	persuaded	
supervised	repaired	systemized	

Creative	Financial	Helping	Research
conceptualized	administered	assessed	clarified
created	analyzed	coached	evaluated
designed	balanced	counseled	identified
established	budgeted	diagnosed	inspected
fashioned	forecast	facilitated	organized
illustrated	marketed	represented	summarized
invented	planned		
performed	projected		

The Talent Bank

Once a resume is completed, it can be fed into the Talent Bank, now available in many local Job Service offices. The Bank is an electronically searchable database of resumes or other statements of qualification from job hunters seeking employment. Those searching for jobs or new opportunities can post their resumes/qualifications to the bank. Employers search the banks to select a group of resumes for further screening.

COMMON QUESTIONS ABOUT RESUMES

What is the purpose of a resume?
To obtain an interview. This can be quite a challenge since the average resume receives only 5-7 seconds of viewing. No one is ever hired solely on the basis of how they look on paper. The resume is your promotional literature for selling yourself. It serves to whet an employer's appetite and make him or her want to know more about you.

How do I accomplish that purpose?
By providing the most relevant information in as concise a manner as possible: the most positive, impressive highlights from your past that would be applicable to the position you seek.

What's a good way to start?
Describing yourself on paper is difficult and somewhat dehumanizing. Make a list of information about yourself, set it aside and add to it later. Place the accumulated data in a format that best emphasizes your strengths and delete the least relevant information.

What's important to emphasize?
Focus on what you have achieved and learned and not just on how and where you have spent your time. Be as specific as possible in citing examples to support your statements. Emphasize only your very best side, the information most applicable to the job at hand. Use only the most impressive tip of the iceberg that also relates to the employer's needs. Editing is difficult, but be sure not to bury the most relevant and attractive information in too much irrelevant detail.

I feel like I'm bragging.
There's no room for modesty in a job search. Employers expect to see ideal candidates, and those who don't portray themselves as such are seldom given the benefit of the doubt. Don't lie, but don't sell yourself short. Save being humble for the interview.

Is tone important in a resume?
Tone is the personality that comes through on a resume—sentence structure, word usage, etc. It can say as much about you as the content.

What is a "statement of objective?"
This is a sentence or two at the beginning of your resume that tells a prospective employer at a glance if you are a possible match for their needs. It is both general, so as to not exclude you from openings you might be interested in, yet specific, so it does communicate some boundaries to the employer. It is essential for individuals with extensive unrelated experience.

What if all my experience is unrelated to my objective?
You might want to summarize the various skills you have learned in past jobs, and emphasize the skills you've acquired that would be relevant in the prospective position. You should consider a functional resume.

What should not be included in a resume?
Information unrelated to your job objective. Also avoid using a picture, height and weight, Social Security number, and other personal information, as well as

misspelled and incorrectly used words, slang or jargon, abbreviations, and flowery or overused adjectives and phrases.

How creative should I be?

Try to be somewhat creative, but you want your resume to stand out through its content. Being overly creative with the appearance or format of the resume may turn off some employers.

What else should I know?

Standard length is one page. Avoid using "I" since this is assumed; use action verbs to describe duties and accomplishments. Use different resumes for different job types. Heavier paper gives the resume a more professional look, and be sure it is free of smudges or stray marks. Be sincere, appropriate, and keep the information relevant.

Where do I distribute the resume?

Have the resume prepared to send to all individuals you contact. You can also attach it to applications, and be sure to send a cover letter along with the resume, introducing yourself and describing your experiences to the employer. All your information should be sent to the person you have been in contact with who has the authority to hire you. Be sure to confirm spellings of names and accuracy of titles.

INTERVIEWING

Most hiring decisions are made at the first interview. How you come across in that interview could be as important as your experience and job talents. Here are some interviewing tips that will help you get the job you want:

Before the Interview

- Learn as much as you can about the company salary and benefits. Friends, neighbors and relatives who work for the company are good sources of information. Libraries, local chambers of commerce, etc. are also helpful.
- Learn everything you can about the job and how your previous experience and training qualify you for the job.
- Write down the things you will need to complete applications (background and experience list, resume or work summary, samples of work if applicable, etc.)
- Be sure to bring your social security card, driver's license, union card, military records, etc.

The Interview

- Dress for the interview as you would for the job. Don't overdress or look too informal.
- Always go to the interview alone. Arrange for babysitters, transportation and other pitfalls ahead of time so that you can be on time and relaxed in the interview.
- Find common ground with the employer. Pictures, books, plants, etc. in the employer's office can be conversation topics.
- Express your interest in the job and the company using information you gathered to prepare for the interview
- Let the interviewer direct the conversation

- Answer questions in a clear and positive manner. Show how your experience and training will make you productive in the shortest time with minimal supervision.
- Speak positively of former employers and coworkers no matter why you left even if you were fired from your last job
- Let the employer lead into conversation about benefits. Your focus on these items can be a turn off. But, don't be afraid to ask questions about things you really need to know.
- When discussing salary, be flexible—avoid naming a specific salary. If you're too high, you risk not getting the job. If you're too low, you undersell yourself. Answer questions on salary requirements with responses such as, "I'm interested in the job as a career opportunity so I'm negotiable on the starting salary." Negotiate, but don't sell yourself short.

Closing the Interview
- If the employer does not offer you a job or say when you will hear about it, ask when you may call to find out about the decision
- If the employer asks you to call or return for another interview, make a written note of the time, date and place
- Thank the employer for the interview and reaffirm your interest and qualifications for the job

COMMON QUESTIONS ABOUT INTERVIEWING

What is the objective of an interview?
For the employer, it is to see if your paper image and portrayal stand up in real life: to see if you are a match for the position at hand. Your objective should be to explore whether or not this is a place you'd like to work. Formulate open-ended questions and probe. Look for indicators.

Do I have to dress up?
Yes, although more formal dress is usually most appropriate, gear yourself to the dress standards of the particular workplace. When in doubt, dress up to show you take the interview seriously.

How do I make an impression?
Be yourself. Smile. Use a firm handshake and make frequent eye contact. Elaborate on information from your resume that indicates you will work out well, that there is little risk in hiring you, and that you have a steady, predictable record of dedication. Be confident.

What should I bring?
Extra copies of your resume, and any other items that may be appropriate and relevant to the job. Be sure to provide these items at the proper point of the interview.

What is the best way to prepare?
List all the questions you think will be asked, talk to someone in the field or in a similar position, role-play with a friend or roommate, or any other activity that you feel will help you prepare.

How do I get information about the position or interviewer, or both?

Many firms are willing to send you a job description if you ask for one. It is possible to get a wealth of information about companies and even individuals on the Internet, or even from a library. College placement offices also have brochures, reports and other related information.

How do I get information during an interview?

You will always be given a chance to ask questions. Remember, though, that good interviewers will control the interview so that they first get all the information they want about you before they tell you too much about the job. In this way they avoid "telegraphing"—revealing the "right" answers to their questions.

How can I get them talking first?

After you answer a question, ask one. This will make the interview more conversational and natural. Ask open-ended questions like "In what direction is the company moving?" or "How would a typical day on the job be spent?"

What other techniques might the interviewer use?

If the interviewer has been trained well, he or she might "funnel" questions from general to specific—meaning they may begin by asking about general experience with customer service, followed by asking of any particular instances or bad experiences and how you handled them specifically.

How honest should I be?

Be honest, but not blunt. Don't offer negative information that is unnecessary or irrelevant. At the same time, you'll fit in best if you leave no surprises, especially about your abilities.

What if I'm asked a question I can't answer?

You more than likely will not be quizzed during your interview. A question that throws you can be handled by asking for clarification or an example, and if you still do not know, say so. However, too many "I don't knows" may indicate you failed to do enough preparation.

Will I be asked any trick questions?

Maybe. They will probably be concerned with how serious you are about this career, profession and particular job. They may ask about other alternatives or positions you may be considering, to which you want to appear as though you are focusing on this job exclusively. A common response by you may be, "Since this is exactly what I'm looking for, I've postponed looking at other positions. If I'm not accepted, I would probably check with (competitor)." Be aware that some employers have in mind certain answers or responses to certain questions that may disqualify you, so be careful how you field questions regarding future plans, other jobs, etc.

What should I ask about?

Whatever is necessary to meet your criteria for selection, and to give you a good feel for the job, the people and the working environment. Some topics to ask about are responsibilities, time commitments, co-workers, travel, style of management, the selection process, etc. Find out what your first day, week and month would be like on the job, and be able to explain how you would approach these responsibilities.

What questions will likely be asked?

The following is a list of common questions taken from interview evaluation forms and used frequently by many employers:

Why should I hire you?
What are your current job expectations?
Describe your educational background.
What was your favorite course in school? Why?
Describe the previous jobs you have had, beginning with your most recent.
What were your major responsibilities in your last job?
What are some of the things you did particularly well in your last job? Or achieved the greatest success in?
Why did you leave your last job?
What were some of the negative qualities of your last job?
What did you like most/least about your past jobs and academic work?
Describe something you did that was not normally part of your job.
Do you like working with figures?
What do you think are the qualities of a good supervisor?
What do you consider to be the perfect job for you?
What do you feel have been your most significant accomplishments?
Give an accurate description of yourself.
Would you have any trouble making it to work by 8:00 a.m.?
Describe what you see as your major strengths and weaknesses for the position.
Are there certain things you feel more confident about doing? What are they, and why do you feel the way you do?
If you had a choice of responsibilities within this department, which would you prefer?
How do you perceive your role in interacting with other department members?
What key factors attract you to this position or company?
What do you see yourself doing in five years?
How much independence and flexibility do you like in a job?
What do you expect for a starting salary?
When can you start?

TESTING

For some jobs, you may need to take a test. Usually, the job announcement or ad will say if a test is required. There are several types of selection and job fitness tests:

- Aptitude tests predict how easily you will learn the job and how well you perform job tasks
- Job knowledge and proficiency tests measure what you know and what you can do in a job (for example, word processing speed for a secretary job, knowledge of street names and routes for a firefighter job, etc.)
- Literacy tests measure reading and arithmetic levels
- Personality tests help identify your personal style in dealing with tasks and other people. Certain personalities can be well suited for some jobs and not so well suited for other jobs. For example, an outgoing person may be well suited for a sales job.
- Honesty and Integrity tests evaluate the likelihood of stealing and trustworthiness of applicants
- Physical ability tests measure strength, flexibility, stamina and speed for jobs that require physical performance
- Medical examinations and tests determine physical fitness to do a job
- Drug tests show the presence of illegal drugs that could impair job performance and threaten the safety of others

How to Prepare for Tests

You can't study directly for aptitude tests. But you can get ready to do your best by learning as much as you can about the test by taking other tests. Look for tests or quizzes in magazines and school books. Set time limits. By taking tests, you learn about the testing process. This will help you feel more comfortable when you are tested.

Brush up on your skills. For example, if you are taking a typing test, practice typing. If you're taking a construction test, review books and blueprints. Get ready for physical tests by doing activities similar to those required for the job. For literacy tests, review and do exercises in reading and math books or enroll in remedial classes.

It's natural to be nervous about tests (some anxiety may even help you). Here are some tips that will help you take most tests:

1. Make a list of what you need for the test (pencil, eyeglasses, ID, etc.) Check it before leaving.
2. Get a good night's sleep
3. If you're sick, call and reschedule the test
4. Leave for the test site early
5. If you have any physical difficulties, tell the test administrator
6. If you don't understand the test instructions, ask for help before the test begins
7. If there are strict time limits, budget the time. Don't linger on difficult questions.
8. Find out if guessing is penalized. If not, guess on questions you're not sure about.
9. If you have time, review your answers. Check to make sure you did not misread a question or make careless mistakes.
10. You may be able to re-take the test. Ask about the re-testing policy.
11. Get a proper interpretation of your scores. The scores may indicate other career opportunities that should be pursued.

AFTER THE INTERVIEW

Make each interview a learning experience. After it's over, ask yourself these questions:

- What points did I make that seemed to interest the employer?
- Did I present my qualifications well? Did I overlook qualifications that were important for the job?
- Did I learn all I needed to know about the job?
- Did I ask questions I had about the job?
- Did I talk too much? Too little?
- Was I too tense? Too relaxed?
- Was I too aggressive? Not aggressive enough?
- Was I dressed appropriately?
- Did I effectively close the interview?

Make a list of specific ways you can improve your next interview. Remember, "practice makes perfect" – the more you interview the better you will get at it.

If you plan carefully and stay motivated, you can "market your job talents." You will get a job that uses your skills and pays you well.

JOB SEARCH CHECKLIST

Complete items 1-3 on the checklist before starting your job search
Complete items 4-5 every day of your search
Complete items 6-9 when you have interviews

1. Identify Occupations
   - Make a background and experience list
   - Review information on jobs
   - Identify jobs that use your talents

2. Identify Employers
   - Ask friends, relatives, etc. to help you look for job openings
   - Go to your State Employment Service Office for assistance
   - Contact employers to get company and job information
   - Utilize other sources to get job leads
   - Obtain job announcements and descriptions

3. Prepare Materials
   - Write resumes – use job announcements to match your skills with job requirements
   - Write cover letters or applications
   - Assemble a job search kit (pens, maps, guides, background list, etc.)
   - Use the Talent Bank

4. Plan Your Time
   - Wake up early to start looking for work
   - Make a "to do" list of everything you'll do to look for a job
   - Work hard all day to find a job
   - Reward yourself

5. Contact Employers
   - Call employers directly (even if they're not advertising openings)
   - Talk to the person who would supervise you if you were hired
   - Go to companies to fill out applications
   - Contact friends and relatives to see if they know about openings
   - Use America's Job Bank on the Internet

6. Prepare for Interviews
   - Learn about the company you're interviewing with
   - Review job announcements to determine how your skills will help you do the job
   - Assemble resumes, forms, etc.

7. Go to Interviews
   - Dress right for the interview – go alone
   - Be clean, concise, positive
   - Thank the interviewer

8. Evaluate Interviews
   - Send a hand-written thank you note to the interviewer within 24 hours
   - Think about how you could improve the interview

9. Take Tests
   - Find out about the test(s) you will be taking
   - Brush up on job skills
   - Relax and be confident

10. Accept the Job!
    - Understand job duties and expectations, work hours, salary, benefits, etc.
    - Be flexible when discussing salary (but don't sell yourself short)
    - Congratulations!

THE MOST COMMON JOB-HUNTING MISTAKES

1. Not taking action – Putting off decisions, phone calls, leads, writing, looking. Not doing anything constructive. Avoiding even thinking about doing something. Making excuses, limiting yourself, erecting roadblocks to progress, complaining and generally procrastinating.

2. Not reflecting enough – Not thinking about what is wanted, ideal or possible. Jumping to the search and jumping too often to the wrong job, simply because it appeared first.

3. Not taking advantage of all potential resources – Overlooking the assistance and leads that can be found in talking with friends, parents, professors, etc. Not using libraries or the Internet. Hesitating to call people you don't know.

4. Not exploiting skills and experience – Not understanding the unique value, strengths and marketability of your past.

5. Not being committed to the job search – Not making adequate time for preparing and searching, or not giving it the highest priority.

6. Not empathizing with the employer's perspective – The employer has needs, time frames, problems and constraints that may or may not be compatible with yours.

7. Not being positive – Underestimating the power of attitude on the process and the employer.

8. Not anticipating and practicing for an interview – Not being able to relate your abilities to the employer's needs. Not role-playing and formulating a strategy for success.

9. Not following up in a professional manner – Thank-you letters, even after rejection, can make a name for you in what may prove to be a small, closely knit profession.

Below, in rank order, are reasons business and industrial managers gave for not offering a job to a new graduate, based upon a survey by Frank S. Endicott, former Director of Placement of Northwestern University:

1. Poor personal appearance
2. Overbearing know-it-all
3. Inability to express self clearly; poor voice, diction, grammar
4. Lack of planning for career; no purpose or goals
5. Lack of confidence and poise
6. Lack of interest and enthusiasm
7. Failure to participate in activities
8. Overemphasis on money; interest only in best dollar offer
9. Poor scholastic record—just got by
10. Unwilling to start at the bottom—expects too much too soon
11. Makes excuses, evasiveness, hedges on unfavorable factors in records
12. Lack of tact
13. Lack of maturity
14. Lack of courtesy
15. Condemnation of past employers
16. Lack of social understandings
17. Marked dislike for school work
18. Lack of vitality
19. Fails to look interviewer in the eye
20. Limp, fishy handshake
21. Indecision
22. Loafs during vacations preferring lakeside pleasures
23. Unhappy married life
24. Friction with parents
25. Sloppy application blank
26. Merely shopping around
27. Only wants a job for short time
28. Little sense of humor
29. Lack of knowledge of field of specialization
30. Parents make decision for them
31. No interest in company or industry
32. Emphasis on who they know
33. Unwillingness to go where we sent them
34. Cynical
35. Low moral standards
36. Lazy
37. Intolerant with strong prejudices
38. Narrow interests
39. Spends much time in movies
40. Poor handling of personal finances
41. No interest in community activities
42. Inability to take criticism
43. Lack of appreciation of value of experience
44. Radical ideas
45. Late to interview without good reason
46. Never heard of company
47. Failure to express appreciation for interviewer's time
48. Asks no questions about the job
49. High-pressure type
50. Indefinite response to questions

COMMON QUESTIONS ABOUT THE FOLLOW-UP

How important is the thank-you letter?
Thank-you letters have been found to be the only correlation between people who are looking for positions and those who get hired. They've been found to correlate even more than qualifications, amount of experience or degree of interest.

What is involved in a good thank-you letter?
This is usually personal, explaining your interest in the position, referring to a topic which was discussed, or providing more indicators of how well you'll fit in. More information about your qualifications, an example of your work and alternative solutions to a problem which you learned of during the interview would all be appropriate. This letter serves to concisely remind them of you at the time of the employment decision.

When should I send it?
You should send a hand-written letter within 24 hours of the interview.

Is timing important?
Yes. Most job processes, including selections and applicant review, are RANDOM. The most qualified applicant is often buried beneath those who were a bit more aggressive and marketed themselves more effectively. Hence, the more leads you pursue, the greater chance of success.

How can I be persistent without being overbearing?
Proper follow-up is more a matter of the right timing, not the quantity of contacts. Ask when the decision is being made, or check back when you feel they've reviewed your resume or are making the hiring decision after your interview.

What should I do if I think I'm being stalled?
Employers often put an applicant on hold. This may be because they are waiting for final approval of the position or because they think they can attract more qualified applicants if they delay. You can force the issue subtly by alluding to another job offer, or you can be more blatant by giving a date by which you need to know. Either method indicates you have a sense of value and self-worth and are not willing to be put off. Be careful not to appear too demanding though.

I was rejected, but I have no idea why.
Chances are small that you'll ever be given the real reason. If you felt you had a good chance, you should persist and acquire information that can help you for your next interview.

AFTER YOU ARE HIRED

- Come to closure with hanging leads – Contact any employers who are still considering you and tell them you've found a job, and thank them for their interest. Regardless of the profession you choose, you can be certain it is a tight network. You may want to work for one of those employers later, or keep in contact with them in your current position.
- Learn to listen
- Learn the background of your area – The history of the people and the development of departmental responsibilities can help give you indicators of

- the written and unwritten "rules" of the field, and what changes can be expected.
- Learn the informal power network – Bear in mind that power is often outside the formal structure. Who is respected and who is not? Whose opinion of you is going to matter more than anything you do?
- Make time for people as well as the task – Focus on doing a good job, but also be sure to concentrate on developing good relationships with those you work with. Both are important. Be sensitive to your place within the hierarchy.
- Be sensitive to processes – What may seem slow or inefficient might serve a valuable purpose that is not initially apparent. Learn through observing.
- Keep the right attitude and perspective – Be appreciative of the opportunity long after you are hired. No matter what may be asked of you, try to treat each assignment as a learning experience.
- Use your resources to their fullest potential – Take advantage of all the options available to you to learn in your current environment. Taking part in projects and committees can be beneficial and show you are interested. Learn all you can as soon as you can.

HOW TO PREPARE FOR A CIVIL SERVICE EXAMINATION

This pamphlet will introduce you to civil service examinations. You will get some advice on preparing for written tests. You will also see sample written test questions.

First, we would like to give you some background. WHY A TEST?

The State Constitution says that public employees must be hired for jobs on the basis of their merit and fitness. The constitution also says that examinations have to be used to measure merit and fitness for most jobs.

In practical terms, *merit and fitness* means finding people who are best suited to a particular job. The idea is to hire people who will be able to do the job well. In fact, the State is no different from private companies. Any employer wants workers who can do a good job.

There are several ways to find good workers. When private companies hire, they ask people what kind of work they have done in the past and how they would do the company's job. They also look at resumes and school records. Sometimes they give tests.

Through civil service examinations, the State does many of the same things in a structured way that private companies do when they hire.

Written and oral tests are designed to find out how people would do the State's job. Evaluation of training and experience is a detailed look at applications and resumes. Performance tests are tasks that measure certain skills, like typing or entering data at computer terminals.

All examinations are based on the kind of job to be filled. The major difference between examinations and other ways of hiring is that examinations all use some kind of formal rating scale or system that is as fair and objective as possible. Each candidate for an examination answers the same questions or does the same task. In any test, all candidates receive a score (rating) based on the same factors. This helps make sure that everyone has a fair and equal chance to get a job and it helps the State find the people best suited to the available jobs. This is the why behind examinations.

HOW EXAMINATIONS ARE DEVELOPED

Before there is an examination for any job, the Department of Civil Service takes a good look at the job to find out what tasks and duties it involves. Civil Service staff may do any or all of these:

- Ask employees and their supervisors to fill out questionnaires
- Ask employees to make lists of the tasks they do during a day, week, or month
- Observe employees while they are working
- Interview employees
- Interview supervisors and program directors

After getting a clear picture of the job, Civil Service staff meets with agency staff where the job exists. They decide what type of examination would measure how well candidates are suited to the job. An examination may have more than one part. For example, there may be a written part to cover some aspects of the job and an oral part to cover others. Each part of an examination is called a test.

Once the examination is planned, experts in the job field help develop test questions and rating scales.

WHAT EXAMINATION ANNOUNCEMENTS TELL YOU

Announcements are published for all civil service examinations. You can find out what examinations are coming up by checking with the Department of Civil Service, the State Job Service, local libraries, or placement offices.

When you pick up an announcement, you should read it carefully.

Find out what jobs are available.

The announcement will tell you the job title, typical job duties, and where the jobs are. Here is an example from an announcement for Compensation Claims Clerk:

As a Compensation Claim Clerk, you would perform responsible clerical work in the development and processing of workers' compensation and disability benefits claims cases with the State Insurance Fund. Under supervision, you would organize and determine priority of claims bills; pay certain bills; review claim files; consult appropriate manuals, guidelines, and schedules to determine if treatment is reasonable; verify ratings and compute allowable fees; complete vouchers; and respond to inquiries by doctors, billing offices, and claimants concerning the status of bills. You would also recommend arbitration of disputed fees when appropriate.

The description of the job duties helps people decide if they want to be a Compensation Claims Clerk. Such a clerk should like to:
- Work with numbers (pay bills, complete vouchers)
- Compare facts and figures (*review claim files, consult appropriate manuals, guidelines, and schedules to determine if treatment is reasonable*)
- Keep records and make routine decisions (*organize and determine the priority of claims bills, recommend arbitration of disputed fees*)
- Write to members of the public or talk to them by phone (*respond to doctors, billing offices, and claimants concerning the status of bills*)

Think about what you would like to do. If a job on an announcement looks interesting to you, read further.

Find out which jobs are open to you.

There are minimum qualifications for most jobs. These tell you the kind of background you must have before you can take the examination. Here are the minimum qualifications for Compensation Claims Clerks:

MINIMUM QUALIFICATIONS: On or before the date of the written test, candidates must meet the following requirements:

Either I — High school diploma or possession of high school equivalency diploma issued by an appropriate educational authority or other high school level diploma;

or II — Four years of office, business, industrial, or other work experience which involved public contact; or military experience. Each completed year of high school study (grades 9-12) may be substituted for one year of work experience

For many examinations, there is more than one way to meet the minimum qualifications. A candidate for Compensation Claims Clerk needs either a high school diploma or four years of work experience, but not both. A person who has two years of high school study and two years of work experience also qualifies.

Be sure you meet the minimum qualifications before you decide to apply for an examination. Many examinations require an application fee that will not be returned. If you do not have the minimum qualifications, you will not be able to take the examination or get a fee refund.

Find out what the examination will be like.

There will be a part of the announcement marked selection. It will tell you whether to expect a written test, an oral test, an evaluation of training and experience or a combination of tests.

This is the selection part of the Compensation Claims Clerk announcement:

SELECTION: There will be a written test which candidates must pass in order to be considered for appointment. The written test will be designed to test for knowledge, skills and/or abilities in such areas as:
- Arithmetic computation
- Arithmetic reasoning
- Understanding and interpreting written material

What does this announcement tell you?

First, the examination will have a written test only - there will be no oral test, no rating of training and experience.

Second, the test will cover a limited number of areas.

People hired to be Compensation Claims Clerks must have enough knowledge and skill in these areas to do the job. In other words, these are critical areas. They may not be the only critical areas, but they are the only ones covered by this test.

If you:
- are interested in the job
- meet the minimum qualifications, and
- wish to take the examination,

be sure to send in an application. Then you can begin to get ready for the examination.

HOW TO PREPARE FOR AN EXAMINATION

Before you get ready for the examination, read the selection part of the announcement again. There are certain words that appear often in lists of examination subject areas:
- principles, practices, procedures, methods, techniques
- understanding, interpreting, applying, reasoning, solving

The first set of words is usually a sign that you will be asked about your knowledge of a given subject. The second set of words usually indicates that you will be tested for a skill or an ability. You would prepare differently for a test of knowledge than for a test of skill.

Preparing for a Test of Knowledge

If you are going to be tested for your knowledge, you can
- read books, magazines, manuals or other printed material
- ask people who know a lot about the subject for information
- rely on your own background

Try your local library first for books and magazines. If the public library does not have the kinds of books you need, a nearby school or college may. You can go there and take notes. Sometimes you can borrow the books (with the help of your public library) through inter-library loan. Some libraries have collections of government documents. Books or manuals available at your present job may be useful also.

Sometimes people who are familiar with the job can be helpful. They may be able to answer your questions, recommend books to read or help you focus your studying on areas that matter.

HOW TO TAKE MULTIPLE-CHOICE TESTS

When the selection portion of an examination announcement says, *There will be a written test;* you can usually expect multiple-Choice questions. For example:

Which one of the following trees is an evergreen?
   A. Maple   B. Oak   C. Birch   D. Pine

Only one of the four answer choices is correct; the others are wrong in some way or another. The answer to the question is choice *D, pine*. Its needles stay green all year. The other choices - maple, oak, and birch - are trees that lose their leaves in the fall.

Not all multiple-choice questions ask for simple facts. Some require you to solve problems or choose the best course of action for a given situation. The question below is intended for Mental Hygiene Therapy Aide Trainees.

A Therapy Aide Trainee's job is to help people who are. mentally ill or mentally retarded learn to get along in the community outside facilities or institutions. This means showing them how to care for themselves, how to get along with other people, how to solve problems they have at the moment. When a Therapy Aide acts, he or she has to think about what is best for the person being helped. This question is designed to test for good judgment in working with mentally retarded people.

George is a mentally retarded adult who is staying in the building where you work. He is getting ready to go outside for a walk and has buttoned his jacket the wrong way. What is best for you to do?
   A. Tell George to button his jacket the right way before he goes outside.
   B. Ask George to wait while you button his jacket the right way.
   C. Show George how to button his jacket the right way and help him do it.
   D. Let George wear his jacket the way he buttoned it.

The answer is choice C. The best way to help George is to show him how to button his jacket correctly. This is something he would have to be able to do for himself if he were living in the community.

Choice A is wrong because it does not give George any help. It assumes that George knows how to button his jacket correctly, but he may not. If George does not understand how to button his jacket, just telling him to do it right will not be enough.

Choice D is wrong also. Most people do not go outside with their jackets buttoned incorrectly. It looks sloppy and can be embarrassing.

Choice B is wrong because it does not allow George to do anything for himself. George will learn best by buttoning the jacket the right way, with help.

Behavior that is not acceptable for other people is not acceptable for George either.

We'll give you more samples of multiple-choice questions later. First here is some general information and advice.

1. READ THE INSTRUCTIONS
   Be sure you understand them before you start on the questions.

2. READ THE QUESTIONS CAREFULLY
   Make sure you are reading what is printed in the test booklet - not what you expect to see or want to see. Read the questions carefully, and then read each choice
   - Read all choices
   - Make sure you understand each choice before you decide which answer is best
   - Pick out the one choice that BEST answers the question. The best choice will be the one that tell what people in the job should do most of the time.
   - Answer the question as it is asked in the booklet. Do not assume the question means something it does not say.

3. USE YOUR TIME WISELY
   You will have a certain amount of time to take the test. Unless you are taking a speed test (more about those later), the time allowed should be plenty for you to read and answer the questions carefully. You should not waste time, though. Keep working through the test

4. ANSWER THE EASY QUESTIONS FIRST, BUT ANSWER EVERY QUESTION You get just as much credit for an easy question as for a hard one. Do not take too much time at first on the hard questions. Answer all the easy questions. Then, in the time left over, go back and figure out the hard ones. IF YOU SKIP A QUESTION, MAKE SURE THAT YOU LEAVE THAT SPACE OPEN ON THE ANSWER SHEET.

5. DO NOT BE AFRAID TO GUESS IF YOU ARE NOT ABSOLUTELY SURE OF THE ANSWER
   - If you do not answer a question, you will not get credit for it. Generally, if you guess correctly, you will get credit.
   - If you are sure a choice is wrong, stop thinking about that choice. The questions have four possible answers. Most people see right away that one or two of those answers cannot be correct. Stop thinking about that one or two, and just think about the others.
   - Choose the best of the choices that remain. Even if one choice seems only a little better than the other one or two, pick that one. The difference between a right answer and a wrong one can sometimes seem very small.

6. BE AWARE OF KEY WORDS

This section will show you some of the words to watch for when you read multiple-choice questions.

Best, greatest, least, and *most* show up in questions like *Which one of the following is the BEST way to do X?* or *Which one of the following is the most effective way to prepare Y?* These words are signs to be very careful when you read the answer choices. Do not settle for the first choice that looks good to you. There may be a better answer to the question.

Question: Of the following foods, which one is the best source of vitamin C?

Answer Choices:
- A. One cup of grapefruit juice
- B. One cup of sliced peaches
- C. One cup of mashed potatoes
- D. One cup of chopped broccoli

Explanation: All of these foods contain some vitamin C. Many people know that citrus fruits, like oranges, grapefruit, and lemon, are good sources of vitamin C. That makes choice A look attractive. But one cup of broccoli actually contains more vitamin C than one cup of grapefruit juice. Choice D is the correct answer. People who work in nutrition - those who would see this kind of question on a test - should recognize that while choice A is a good answer, it is not the best answer. These people need to know more than most about vitamins and minerals in food so they can plan menus for others.

Pay attention to phrases like *Which one of the following*. This means that you should concentrate on the answer choices that are listed. If you can think of another answer that might be possible some time or other, do not worry about it. When the question says *Which one of the following*, you can expect a best answer among those listed.

Words like *common, generally, likely, more, often, primarily, probably, typical,* and *usual* are reminders to look for the choice you would select most of the time. Do not choose one that would only be correct on rare occasions.

Question: Which one of the following is generally the best way to repair an X machine?

Answer choice:
- A. Replace the entire engine
- B. Replace the valves
- C. Rewire the starter
- D. Replace the gaskets and add oil to the reservoir

Explanation: Suppose that in 99 cases out of 100, rewiring the starter will solve the problem. Then choice C is generally the best way to do the repair. This is the correct answer. Remember, nearly every rule has an exception. Questions that use words like generally and usually are looking for the rule, not the exception.

Watch for words like disadvantage, except, least, and not. Questions using these words are looking for an exception. If the question asks about a disadvantage, be sure not to choose an advantage as your answer. Be careful of words beginning with non- or un-. Non- and un- are ways of saying not.

Question:	If grease in a pan catches fire, it is unwise to do which one of the following?
Answer Choice:	A. Cover the pan with a lid B. Pour water on the fire
Explanation:	Covering the pan with a lid would smother the fire by cutting off the oxygen it needs to burn. Pouring water on the fire would probably make the fire spread and get worse, because water and grease do not mix. So it is unwise to pour water on the fire. Therefore, choice B is the correct answer to the question being asked. When tests include questions like this, it is because people doing the job must know what actions would cause trouble as well as what actions would solve problems.

When a question uses the word first, look for a set of events to put in order.

Question:	Which one of the following should you do first if X happens?
Answer Choices:	A. Call the security staff B. Turn off the power C. Have people leave the area D. Call your supervisor
Explanation:	Suppose that all four choices list actions that should be taken. The important thing to know is what to do first in the situation. Let's say X is a life-threatening situation. The first thing to do then is to have people leave the area. That is the correct answer. But maybe X is not life-threatening. Maybe you would have people leave only when a repair crew arrives, so the crew would have room to work. Then one of the other choices - turn off the power, perhaps would be correct.

When you see a question like this, be sure you understand the situation thoroughly. Then figure out which choices would be first, second, third, fourth. When you think you have the right order, mark down your first choice as the answer. The reason for doing it this way is to make sure you think about the whole series of events, not just one event by itself. You are more likely to choose the correct answer that way.

HOW TO TAKE SPEED TESTS
The speed tests we mentioned earlier are usually only a part of longer tests. The test instructions will tell you if you will be taking a speed test. This kind of test will be in a separate booklet with a separate time limit.

A speed test is designed to determine how accurate you can be when you are working rapidly. The test monitor will tell you how much time you have to work on the questions, and will collect the booklet when the time is up. So if you are taking a speed test, you should work as quickly as possible and skip any question if you are not sure of the answer. On a speed test, you are not expected to answer all the questions, but you are expected to answer correctly all of the questions you attempted. If you have time, go back and answer any questions you skipped.

———

HOW TO PREPARE FOR THE BASIC SKILL SUBJECTS
ARITHMETIC, VOCABULARY, GRAMMAR, SUPERVISION

Preparing for an examination is an individual process. It depends on the job description, examination announcement, and on your own knowledge and skills. A study of previous examinations and the examination announcement should give you an idea of the kinds of questions you may get; however, developing the various skills in arithmetic, grammar, vocabulary, and supervision needed to answer the questions can be done only by you.

We have listed below some examples relating to these skills which you may need to pass a clerical/supervisory examination. Work out the examples below; if you have difficulty with any one of them, you know that you should definitely go further into the subject. Even if you can do these examples easily, you should review previous examinations for other kinds of problems that may give you difficulty. In any case, you should determine the areas in which you are weak and concentrate your efforts on them. After doing these questions, see whether your answers and methods match the solutions and key answers at the end of this section.

I. ARITHMETIC

1. An office is 12 feet long and 15 feet wide. What will be the cost of covering the floor wall to wall with carpet that sells for $9.00 a square yard.

2. A stenographer spends 13 hours typing, 4 hours taking dictation, and one-fifth of the time filing. What percentage of her time does she spend on miscellaneous duties if she works a 40-hour week?

3. A clerk, who can do 2¼% of a card-filing job in one hour, works at the rate of 630 cards per hour. How many card must he file to complete the job?

Were you able to do the above easily? In preparing for an examination which may include arithmetic problems, it is essential that you first review your basic arithmetical operations such as addition, subtraction, multiplication, and division of whole numbers, percentages, fractions, and decimals. A 6th- or 7th-year school text will probably give you all the review you need in these fundamentals. After you review the fundamentals, then apply your knowledge to the kind of questions normally given on the examination for which you are preparing.

II. VOCABULARY

fractious conductive
functional congruous
officious contingent

Did you find these words difficult? If you did, you should do something about improving your vocabulary because these are words that came from previous examinations. Again, it is good to go back to fundamentals. Get into the habit of looking up any word you come across in your reading that you don't know, particularly words that have some relationship to the subject matter of your examination. In examinations for Police Officer, words like duress, indictment, contempt, and deter are used because they have to do, in one form or another, with police action. On the same basis, if you are preparing for a clerical-administrative examination, you should be familiar with the words listed above.

III. GRAMMAR

1. Entering the office, the desk was noticed immediately by the visitor.

2. The office manager estimates that the job, which is to be handled by you and I, will require about two weeks for completion.

3. The supervisor knew that the typist was a quiet, cooperative, efficient, employee.

4. We do not know who you have designated to take charge of the new program.

5. Neither Mr. Smith nor Mr. Jones were able to do their assignment on time.

Did you know what was incorrect in the above sentences? These examples came from previous examinations and reflect common errors in grammar and correct usage. If you had any difficulty with these examples, then a review of basic grammatical and punctuation rules is in order. Look through the grammar questions in the examinations included in this book; you will see that certain errors are repeated in each examination. Stress is placed on such principles as agreement between subject and verb, use of the objective form of the pronoun after a preposition, correct use of who or whom, and the punctuation needed for a restrictive or non-restrictive clause. Your studying, therefore, should be geared to a review of these principles.

IV. SUPERVISION

1. Of the following, the one which is NOT a good rule in disciplining subordinates is for a supervisor to
   A. be as specific as possible in criticizing a subordinate for his faults
   B. allow an extended period to elapse after an error has been committed before reprimanding the offending employee
   C. be sure he has all the facts before reprimanding an employee for an error he has committed
   D. reprimand the employee in private even though the fault was committed publicly

2

2. "Unity of command" requires that
    A. all units perform the same operation in the same manner
    B. managers comply with established policy at all times
    C. orders be issued through the established line of authority
    D. managers be in general agreement on policy

3. It is generally best that the greater part of in-service training for the operating employees of an agency in a pubic jurisdiction be given by
    A. a team of trainers from the central personnel agency of the jurisdiction
    B. training specialists on the staff of the personnel unit of the agency
    C. a team of teachers from the public school system of the jurisdiction
    D. members of the regular supervisory force of the agency

4. Studies of organizations show that formal employee participation in the formulation of work policies before they are put into effect is most likely to result in
    A. a reduction in the length of time required to formulate the policies
    B. an increase in the number of employees affected by the policies
    C. a reduction in the length of time required to implement the policies
    D. an increase in the number of policies formulated within the organization

Did you understand what supervisory principles were involved in the above examples? If not, then a review of supervision is in order. Examinations tend to stress the role of a supervisor as a leader who has understanding of human relations and leadership principles. If you feel a need for a refresher in this area, almost any one of the books on this area listed in our catalog should be of help to you.

SOLUTIONS/EXPLANATIONS OF ANSWERS

I. **ARITHMETIC**

1. This problem requires you to know the basic formula for measuring the area of a rectangle (Area = Length x Width) and involves the elementary arithmetical processes of multiplication and division.

   First, change the dimensions from feet to yards because the statement indicates that the cost is to be expressed in yards. Since there are 3 feet in a yard, divide the number of feet by 3 to get yards.

   $$\frac{12 \text{ ft. wide}}{3 \text{ ft. in a yard}} = 4 \text{ yards} \qquad \frac{15 \text{ ft. long}}{3 \text{ ft. in a yard}} = 5 \text{ yards}$$

   4 yards x 5 yards = 20 sq. yards needed
   x$9.00 cost per square yard
   $180.00 cost to cover floor wall to wall

2. This problem requires you to know how to use fractions and how to convert fractions to percentages.

   First, find in hours the equivalent of "1/5 of the time filing."

   (Multiplying by a fraction) 1/5 x 40 hrs. = time filing = 8
   1/5 x 40 hrs. = 8 hrs. filing
   13 hrs. typing
   4 hrs. dictation
   25 hrs. for above duties

   40 hrs. work
   -25 hrs. accounted for, as above
   15 hrs. for miscellaneous duties

   $$\frac{15}{40} = 3/8$$

   (To get % multiply the fraction x 100) $3/8 \times 100 = \frac{300}{8} = 37\frac{1}{2}\%$

3. Rephrase the statement in your mind to read 2¼% of the total equals 6t30 cards.
   If 630 cards are done in 1 hour, and that represents 2¼% of the total number of cards, then

   2¼% of total = 630
   or
   $\frac{9}{4}$% of total = 630

4

(Change percent to fraction by dividing by 100)

$$\frac{9}{400} \text{ of total} = 630$$

$$\text{Total} = 630 \times \frac{400}{9}$$

$$\text{Total} = \frac{252000}{9}$$

$$\text{Total} = 28000 \text{ cards}$$

II. VOCABULARY

The improvement of vocabulary requires intensive and extensive study of words and their meanings.

It is impossible to treat this area adequately in this brief overview.

The best preparation is to secure the book on vocabulary, listed under the heading Basic/General Education, in this catalog.

III. GRAMMAR

1. This sentence is incorrect because we don't know who entered the office. The sentence, as it stands, has a dangling participle, "entering." It indicates that the desk entered the office, which, obviously, is not so. It would be correct to say "Entering the office, the visitor noticed the desk immediately." Then, there is no question about who entered the office.

2. As you probably noted, the sentence should have read "you and me" following the preposition by instead of "you and I." Prepositions such as by, between, etc. are followed by the objective form of the pronoun—me, him, her, us, and them.

3. This sentence has a punctuation error. No comma is ever placed between the adjective and the noun it modifies. The comma after "efficient" is incorrect. The sentence should read: "The supervisor knew that the typist was a quiet, cooperative, and efficient employee."

4. The sentence should have "whom" instead of "who." What is needed is an object to the verb "designated" and, therefore, "whom," the objective form of the pronoun, is used.

5. The sentence is incorrect because the verb "were" should apply to Mr. Jones, the nearer subject. Following a correlative conjunction such as neither-nor or either-or, the verb should be singular.

5

IV. SUPERVISION

1. Answer B: Always remember that in answering a question of this type, three of the four choices will probably be GOOD rules to follow in discipline.

   Answers A, C, and D ARE good so that leaves B.

   B is NOT good rule for several reasons:
   1. If you allow an extended period to elapse, both you and he may have FORGOTTEN the incident.
   2. He'll probably be making more of the same errors.
   3. Discipline, as a corrective device, is most helpful when the incident or error is fresh in the employee's mind.
   4. The employee may wonder why you waited. He may think you are using this instance as a means of "picking on" him for something else he did or for personal dislike.

2. Answer C: Unity of command by DEFINITION means the organizational setup whereby authority and orders follow definite chains or lines of authority. (Look at a typical organization chart.) An important concept associated with this principle is that no member of an organization reports to more than one supervisor.

3. Answer D: Note the wording of the question—"greater part." This question tests your recognition of the principle that one of the supervisor's basic functions is that of employee training and that the regular supervisor in the agency is in the best position to determine what the employee needs to know in order to perform the type, quality, and quantity of work required.

4. Answer C: This answer brings out one of the important forces at work in human relations. People like to participate in preparing plans that may affect them and will, therefore, cooperate more fully in implementing the plans.

GETTING READY FOR TAKING A CIVIL SERVICE EXAM

TABLE OF CONTENTS

What a Civil Service Examination Announcement Tells You 1

    Special Test Administration Needs 1

    Religious Accommodation 1

    Military Personnel 1

How to Apply for a Civil Service Examination 1

Admission Notice 2

On the Day of the Test 2

How to Prepare for the Test 2

Multiple-Choice Question Tips 3

Test Taking Strategies 4

Final Tips 5

Sample Test Questions 6

    Arithmetic Reasoning 7

    Educating and Interacting with the Public 8

    Office Record Keeping 9

    Understanding and Interpreting Written Material 13

State civil service examinations include one or more tests, which are designed to assess candidates' qualifications for jobs to be filled. Many examinations include a written test. A written test presents candidates with questions in a written format, such as multiple-choice, job simulation exercise, constructed-response short answer or essay, or other written test format.

WHAT A CIVIL SERVICE EXAMINATION ANNOUNCEMENT TELLS YOU

Be sure to read the announcement carefully.

The announcement contains important information, such as:

- job title
- date of examination
- job location
- duties
- salary
- description of the test
- deadline date for filing applications
- how to apply
- fee information, if applicable

When a written test is part of the examination, the announcement describes the subject areas or "subtests" that will be covered. If a special test guide is available for the test, the announcement will state that this guide is available and tell you how to access this guide.

The announcement also includes information for candidates who require accommodations or special testing arrangements.

Special Test Administration Needs: Persons with disabilities who require an accommodation to participate in an examination must note this on their applications.

Religious Accommodation: Most written tests are held on Saturdays. If you cannot take the test on the announced test date, due to a conflict with a religious observance or practice, check the box under "Religious Accommodation" on your exam application. They will make arrangements for you to take the test on a different date (usually the following day).

Military Personnel: Candidates wishing to request a military make-up examination for a State examination should contact the State Department of Civil Service's Test Administration Unit.

HOW TO APPLY FOR A CIVIL SERVICE EXAMINATION

The examination announcement will tell you how to apply. You may be able to apply on-line or download the application for your exam. Be sure to carefully follow all instructions provided on the announcement and application. Complete and submit the application by the due date stated on the announcement. For most exams you will be required to pay an application fee.

You are responsible for providing enough information on the application to show that you meet the minimum qualifications for the exam. After you submit your application, the Department will review your qualifications and notify you if you have been approved or disapproved to take the test.

ADMISSION NOTICE

If your exam application is approved, the Department will send you an Admission Notice telling you when and where to report to take the test. If your test is scheduled for more than one test date, the Department will send a separate Admission Notice for each test date.

Allow plenty of time to travel to the test site, to find the correct location and to park, if necessary. Be sure to bring your Admission Notice with you to the test site, along with your photo identification, and two No. 2 pencils. Unless otherwise indicated, you may also bring a quiet, hand-held, solar- or battery-powered calculator and a quiet lunch or snack, if allowed. You will have to present your Admission Notice at the test center, so be sure to bring it with you on the day of the test.

ON THE DAY OF THE TEST

Arrive at the Test Center Early: To be admitted to the test, you must report to the test center on the day and at the time printed on your Admission Notice. If you arrive late, you may not be admitted to the test.

Bring Identification Showing Your Name, Signature and Photograph: Identification Policy: You must bring one piece of current, government-issued identification printed in English, in the name in which you applied to take the test, bearing your photograph and signature.

No Cell Phones or Electronic/Communication Devices at the Test Site: Do NOT bring cell phones, beepers, headphones, or any electronic or other communication devices to the test site. The use of such devices at the test site in the test room, hallways, restrooms, building, grounds, or other areas could result in your disqualification.

No Smoking at the Test Site: Smoking is strictly prohibited at all test centers, including buildings and grounds.

HOW TO PREPARE FOR THE TEST

In most cases, you will have some time between when you apply for an examination and the date of the test. You can use this time to prepare yourself to do your best on the test date. Some general tips to help you prepare for a written, multiple-choice test are presented on the following pages. Some of these tips may help you prepare for other types of tests as well.

Many Civil Service examinations include a written, multiple-choice test. The examination announcement lists the subject areas or "subtests" that the test will cover. Use this information to help prepare for the test.

The four subject areas or "subtests" listed below could be included on a written test for a fictional job title, Services Representative 1: (See the Sample Test Questions included in this guide.)

    Arithmetic Reasoning
    Educating and Interacting with the Public
    Office Record Keeping
    Understanding and Interpreting Written Material

Often, the name of the subject area will give you a good idea about what will be covered in that area. For example, Arithmetic Reasoning would cover solving arithmetic problems that involve addition, subtraction, multiplication, and division.

For most written, multiple-choice tests, the announcement will also include a description of what each subject area will test. For example, a description of the subject area, Arithmetic Reasoning, might be:

> "These questions test for the ability to solve arithmetic problems which are presented in sentence or short paragraph form. Knowledge of addition, subtraction, multiplication, and division is necessary. Questions may also involve the use of percents, decimals, and fractions."

Certain words often appear in the titles and descriptions of subject areas covered in a written test. Some examples include:

- principles, practices, procedures, methods, techniques – These words generally indicate that you will be asked about your knowledge of the principles, practices, procedures, methods, or techniques of the particular subject area.

- understanding, interpreting, applying, reasoning, solving – These words generally indicate that you will be tested for the skill or ability in understanding, interpreting, applying, reasoning, or solving problems or information in the particular subject area.

MULTIPLE-CHOICE QUESTION TIPS

Multiple-choice questions usually include a problem described in a question or incomplete statement and two or more possible answer choices. Read the problem and answer choices carefully. Then, select the one choice that best answers the question or best completes the statement.

Be sure to mark your answer as instructed on the scannable answer sheet provided. For most multiple-choice tests, your score will be based on the total number of questions that you answer correctly.

For most tests, the Department does not take points away from candidates for their wrong answers or apply a "correction for guessing." Therefore, it is to your advantage to answer every question, even if you are not sure which answer is correct.

You should mark only one answer for each question. If you mark more than one answer, that question will be considered incorrect, and you will not receive credit for your answers.

Answering Multiple-Choice Questions:

- Read the entire question carefully and try to answer it without referring to the answer choices.

- Look for any key words in the question that may help you select the correct answer from among the choices. Some common key words are: many, most, least, less, more, good, best, advantage, disadvantage, first, last, never, always, any, not, except, false, and true.

- Always read all of the possible answer alternatives carefully before jumping to the conclusion that a particular one must be the best.

- Use the process of elimination if the correct answer does not immediately occur to you. Eliminate obviously wrong answers and narrow your choice to the ones that directly answer the question. Then select the answer that most exactly answers the question.

- Do not be influenced by the length of the answer choices. The longest answer is not necessarily the correct one.

- Do not select an answer choice just because it includes technical language. Answer choices using technical terminology may be included in order to see whether you know the difference between what "looks right" and what "is right".

- Determine the best answer using only the information supplied in the question, without making unwarranted assumptions. The correct answer is the one that works best for the situation described.

TEST TAKING STRATEGIES

Read all directions, instructions, and test materials carefully. Carefully read and follow all directions and any special instructions for the test. If sample test materials are provided, review them to become familiar with the subject area and format. Read all test materials carefully. Be sure you fully understand the question or problem and the answer choices presented before you select and mark your answer.

Answer all questions designated for your examination(s). At the test site, you will be given Candidate Directions that identify the Test Booklet(s) and question numbers to be completed for each examination.

You are responsible for determining which questions you are to answer, for making sure you have the correct Test Booklet(s), and for completing all test material required for your examination(s).

Mark your answers accurately on the separate, scannable answer sheet. At the test site, you will be given one or more Test Booklet(s) and a separate, scannable answer sheet for each Test Booklet. The completed answer sheets will be scanned and scored by computer. To receive full credit for your answers:

- Use a No. 2 pencil to mark your answers.
- Fill in all identification information required for each answer sheet.
- As you mark your answers, be sure the Test Booklet identified on the answer sheet matches the Test Booklet you are using.
- As you mark your answers, be sure the number and letter of the answer you mark on the answer sheet matches the question you are answering in the Test Booklet.

Budget your time wisely. The total time allowance is based on the amount of test material covered in a group of related examinations or "series." The maximum time allowance for any single test date is eight hours; however, time allowances vary with examination series and yours may be less. If you need to know the total time allowance for your written test before the test date, you may contact this Department for that information.

At the test site, on the day of the test, make note of the total time allowance, the starting and stopping times, and the test materials that you must complete for your examination(s).

After the monitor announces that you may begin the test, you may look over your test materials to help you estimate how much time you will need to complete each part. Keep track of the time as you are working. If you skip over some questions, be sure to come back to them before you complete the test and turn in your test materials.

FINAL TIPS

Before the test:

- Review this guide, the subtest titles, descriptions, and any sample test materials available to familiarize yourself with what the test will cover.
- Study and review the subject areas to be covered on the test.

On the day of the test:

- Allow yourself enough time for traveling to the test site and locating your test room.
- Bring your Admission Notice, two No. 2 pencils, and a photo ID containing your signature, and any other items allowed. ****Please refer to your Admission Notice for items that are allowed.****
- Unless otherwise indicated on your Admission Notice or the examination announcement, you may bring a quiet, hand-held, solar- or battery-powered calculator.
- Do NOT bring any device with a typewriter keyboard, such as a "Spell Checker," "Personal Digital Assistant (PDA)," "Address Book," "Language Translator," "Dictionary," or other similar device to the test site.
- Do NOT bring cell phones, beepers, headphones, or any other communication devices to the test site. The use of such devices at the test site in the test room, hallways, restrooms, building, grounds, or other areas could result in your disqualification.
- Do NOT bring books or reference materials to the test site.
- Do NOT bring this guide or sample test materials to the test site.

During the test:

- Read and follow all directions on your Admission Notice and test administration materials, including candidate directions, test booklets, and answer sheets.
- Follow the monitor's instructions; raise your hand if you have questions or need help.
- Keep track of the time and organize your work accordingly.
- Do not look at the work of other people in the room or you may be disqualified.

After the test:

- Continue to observe test security prohibitions by not removing any test materials from the test room, by not reconstructing or reproducing test materials, and by not discussing the test.

Some Common Sense Suggestions

- Get plenty of rest the night before.
- Dress comfortably, in layers, so you can adapt to the temperature in the test room.
- East breakfast.
- If you are not sure where the test site is, get directions to the site before the test date.
- Leave yourself plenty of time to get to the test site just in case there is traffic, you have car trouble, transportation problems, etc.
- Your attitude and approach to the test will influence how well you perform. A positive attitude will help you do your best.

Samples of the test questions and materials mentioned in this guide are presented on the following pages.

This guide was developed to give you a better understanding of what to expect on a written test. We hope it will help you do your best on your test.

SAMPLE TEST QUESTIONS

Sample questions for the Services Representative 1.

Subjects of Examination on the examination announcement for the Services Representative 1 listed four subject areas:

- Arithmetic Reasoning
- Educating and Interacting with the Public
- Office Record Keeping
- Understanding and Interpreting Written Material

ARITHMETIC REASONING: These questions test for the ability to solve arithmetic problems which are presented in sentence or short paragraph form. Knowledge of addition, subtraction, multiplication, and division is necessary. Questions may also involve the use of percents, decimals, and fractions.

Test Task: For each question, you must read the problem, understand the situation presented, decide what must be done to answer the question, and apply the appropriate arithmetic operation(s), in the correct order, in order to arrive at the correct answer.

Sample Question:

Of the 300 people working at a medical facility, 14% are clerks. How many workers at the medical facility are NOT clerks?

A. 42
B. 86
C. 258
D. 286

Solution: To answer this question correctly, you must first determine what percent of the people working at the medical facility are NOT clerks. Since 14% are clerks, 86% (100% minus 14%) are NOT clerks. You must then convert 86% to its decimal value, 0.86, and multiply 300 by 0.86, to determine what 86% of 300 is (the number of workers at the medical facility who are NOT clerks). Since 300 × 0.86 = 258, the number of workers at the medical facility who are NOT clerks is 258 (choice C).

The correct answer to this sample question is C.

EDUCATING AND INTERACTING WITH THE PUBLIC: These questions test for knowledge of techniques used to interact effectively with individual citizens and/or community groups, to educate or inform them about topics of concern, to publicize or clarify agency programs or policies, to negotiate conflicts or resolve complaints, and to represent one's agency or program in a manner in keeping with good public relations practices. Questions may also cover interacting with others in cooperative efforts of public outreach or service.

Test Task: You will be presented with a variety of situations in which you must apply knowledge of how best to interact with other people.

Sample Question:

A person approaches you expressing anger about a recent action by your department. Which one of the following should be your FIRST response to this person?

A. Interrupt to say you cannot discuss the situation until he calms down.
B. Say you are sorry that he has been negatively affected by our department's action.
C. Listen and express understanding that he has been upset by your department's action.
D. Give him an explanation of the reasons for your department's action.

Solution:

Choice A is not correct. It would be inappropriate to interrupt. In addition, saying that you cannot discuss the situation until the person calms down will likely aggravate him further.

Choice B is not correct. Apologizing for your department's action implies that the action was improper.

Choice C is the correct answer to this question. By listening and expressing understanding that your department's action has upset him, you demonstrate that you have heard and understand his feelings and point of view.

Choice D is not correct. While an explanation of the reasons for the action may be appropriate at a later time, at this moment the person is angry and would not be receptive to such an explanation.

The correct answer to this sample question is choice C.

OFFICE RECORD KEEPING: These questions test your ability to perform common office record keeping tasks. The test consists of two or more "sets" of questions, each set concerning a different problem. Typical record keeping problems might involve the organization or collation of data from several sources; scheduling; maintaining a record system using running balances; or completion of a table summarizing data using totals, subtotals, averages, and percents.

Test Tasks: The test consists of two or more "sets" of questions. Each set involves a different type of problem. Some examples of typical record keeping problems are:

- the organization or collation of data from several sources
- scheduling
- maintaining a record system using running balances
- completion of a table summarizing data using totals, subtotals, averages, and percents

NOTE: Only one type of problem set is presented in this Test Guide for this subject area. The actual test may or may not have a set of this type. It will certainly have at least one set involving a different type of problem.

On the following pages are two tables, three sample questions based on the tables, and the solutions to the questions. Please look at the tables, and read both the questions and the solutions carefully.

DIRECTIONS FOR SAMPLE QUESTIONS: Base your answers to the next three sample questions on the table, "Summary Report of Business Expenses for 2009." Complete as much of the report as you need to answer the sample questions. Use the information given in the summary report itself and in the table, "Report of Business Expenses, 3rd and 4th Quarters." Both tables are shown on the following page.

See the Sample Questions and Solutions on the following pages.

REPORT OF BUSINESS EXPENSES 3RD AND 4TH QUARTERS (26 weeks)				
	3rd Quarter		4th Quarter	
	2009	2008	2009	2008
Payroll Expenses	$55,900	$47,800	$72,700	$65,100
Rental Expenses	22,500	18,900	22,500	18,900
Equipment Expenses				
New Equipment	705	375	5,575	675
Maintenance/Repair	2,860	3,000	3,140	3,400
Utility Expenses				
Electricity	4,850	4,630	4,590	4,450
Heat	130	270	440	410
Employee Benefit Expenses	18,450	15,850	24,100	21,550
Employee Contributions*	*2,500	*2,200	*3,350	*3,040
Total Net Business Expenses*		$8,625		$111,445

*NOTE: Employee Contributions are subtracted from business expenses to obtain Total Net Business Expenses

SUMMARY REPORT OF BUSINESS EXPENSES FOR 2009							
	1st Quarter	2nd Quarter	1st Half	3rd Quarter	4th Quarter	2nd Half	Total For Year
Payroll Expenses	$81,800	$69,300	$151,100			R	
Rental Expenses	22,500	22,500	45,000				
Equipment Expenses	5,235	3,545	8,780				S
Utility Expenses	6,675	5,125	11,800				
Employee Benefit Expenses	26,900	22,900	49,800				
Employee Contributions*	*3,750	*3,200	*6,950				
Total Net Business Expenses* for 2009	139,360	120,170	259,530				
Total Net Business Expenses* for 2008			$231,780			$200,070	
% Change**			V				

*NOTE: Employee Contributions are subtracted from business expenses to obtain Total Net Business Expenses

**NOTE: % Change is the % of increase in Total Net Business Expenses from 2008 to 2009

SAMPLE QUESTION 1:

What is the value of R?
A. $112,900
B. $128,600
C. $137,800
D. None of the above

Solution: To answer this question correctly, you must calculate the value of R (the Payroll Expenses for the 2nd half of 2009).

- The Payroll Expenses for the 3rd and 4th Quarters are shown in the table, "Report of Business Expenses 3rd and 4th Quarters." (Be careful to use the amounts for 2009, and not the amounts for 2008.)
- You must add the Payroll Expenses for the 3rd Quarter of 2009 ($55,900) to the Payroll Expenses for the 4th Quarter of 2009 ($72,700).
  The result is $128,600.

The correct answer to this sample question is choice B, which is $128,600.

SAMPLE QUESTION 2:

What is the value of S?
A. $8,780
B. $15,060
C. $16,230
D. None of the above

Solution: To answer this question correctly, you must calculate the value of S (the total Equipment Expenses for the year 2009).

- You need to understand that Equipment Expenses are expenses for both New Equipment and for Maintenance/Repair.
- The Equipment Expenses for the 3rd and 4th Quarters are shown in the table, "Report of Business Expenses 3rd and 4th Quarters." (Again, be careful to use the amounts for 2009, and not the amounts for 2008.)
- You must add Equipment Expenses for the 3rd Quarter of 2009 ($705 + $2,860) to Equipment Expenses for the 4th Quarter of 2009 ($5,575 + $3,140) in order to calculate Equipment Expenses for the 2nd half of 2009.
- $705 + $2,860 + $5,575 + $3,140 = $12,280
- You must then add Equipment Expenses for the 2nd half of 2009 to Equipment Expenses for the 1st half of 2009, in order to calculate Equipment Expenses for the whole year.
- Equipment Expenses for the 1st half of 2009 are shown in the table, "Summary Report of Business Expenses for 2009."
- $12,280 + 8,780 = $21,060. This is the value of S, the total Equipment Expenses for the year 2009.

Since none of the A, B, or C choices is $21,060, the correct answer to this sample question is choice D, "None of the above."

SAMPLE QUESTION 3:

Which one of the following is closest to the value of V?
A. 10%
B. 11%
C. 12%
D. 28%

Solution: To answer this question correctly, you must calculate the value of V (the percent change in Total Net Business Expenses from the 1st half of 2008 to the 1st half of 2009).

- You must first calculate the amount of change in Total Net Business Expenses from the 1st half of 2009 to the 1st half of 2009.
- Subtract the Total Net Business Expenses for the 1st half of 2008 ($231,780) from the Total Net Business Expenses for the 1st half of 2009 ($259,530).
- The result is $27,750.
- You must then calculate the percent change from the 1st half of 2008 to the 1st half of 2009. Since the percent change is from the 1st half of 2008, the basis of the comparison is the Total Net Business Expenses for the 1st half of 2008.
- Divide the amount of the change by the Total Net Business Expenses for the 1st half of 2008.
- $27,750 divided by $231,780 = .119726, or 11.9726%
- This is closest to 12%.

The correct answer to this sample question is choice C, which is 12%.

UNDERSTANDING AND INTERPRETING WRITTEN MATERIAL: These questions test how well you comprehend written material. You will be provided with brief reading selections and will be asked questions about the selections. All the information required to answer the questions will be presented in the selections; you will not be required to have any special knowledge relating to the subject areas of the selections.

Test Task: For each question, you will be provided with a brief written selection, followed by a question and a set of alternative statements relating to the selection. You must choose the statement that best answers the question. Your answer should be based on the information found in the selection only, NOT on knowledge you may have about the subject from other sources.

Sample Question:

"The increasing demands upon our highways from a growing population and the development of forms of transportation not anticipated when the highways were first built have brought about congestion, confusion, and conflict, until the yearly toll of traffic accidents is now at an appalling level. If the death and disaster that traffic accidents bring throughout the year were concentrated into one calamity, we would shudder at the tremendous catastrophe. The loss is no less catastrophic because it is spread out over time and space."

Which one of the following statements concerning the yearly toll of traffic accidents is best supported by the passage above?
A. It is increasing the demands for safer means of transportation.
B. It has resulted in increased congestion, confusion, and conflict on our highways.
C. It does not shock us as much as it should because the accidents do not all occur together.
D. It has resulted mainly from the new forms of transportation.

Solution: To answer this question correctly, you must evaluate each choice against the written selection and determine the one that is best supported by the written selection.

Choice A: Nowhere in the passage does it say that there has been any demand for safer means of transportation. Someone who picks this choice may believe that there could be or should be a demand for safer transportation, but there is nothing in the passage to base it on. This choice is incorrect.

Choice B: The passage states that it is the congestion, confusion, and conflict which results in the high toll of traffic accidents and not the other way around. A person who picks this choice could either be confused as to which is the cause and which is the effect or not have read the choice carefully. This choice is incorrect.

Choice C: This choice is supported by the last two sentences in the passage. The writer says, "If..., we would shudder." (A shudder is a response to shock.) The implication is that we don't shudder because traffic accidents do not all occur at the same time and place. The writer then points out that we should think of the yearly toll as being catastrophic (shocking) even though the accidents are spread out over time and space. This choice is supported by the information in the passage.

Choice D: There are two reasons given in the passage for the high accident rate. One is the development of new forms of transportation; the other is the increased highway use from a growing population. Neither one is described as the main reason. It is clearly incorrect to say that the new forms of transportation are the main reason. This choice is incorrect.

The correct answer to this sample question is choice C.

HOW TO APPLY FOR CIVIL SERVICE JOBS

TABLE OF CONTENTS

	Page
INSTRUCTIONAL OBJECTIVES	1
CONTENT	1
Introduction	1
1. The Public Service Career Field	1
2. The Employing Agencies	3
3. Choosing a Career Field	4
4. Considering a Public Service Occupation	6
5. Entrance Requirements for the Position	8
6. The Job Application	10
7. The Examination	12
8. The Eligibility List	15
9. Appointment to a Position	17
10. On the Job After Appointment	19
11. The Future of Public Service	20
STUDENT LEARNING ACTIVITIES	21
TEACHER MANAGEMENT ACTIVITIES	22
EVALUATION QUESTIONS	24

HOW TO APPLY FOR CIVIL SERVICE JOBS

INSTRUCTIONAL OBJECTIVES

1. Ability to obtain information on current job opportunities in the various occupational areas found in the public service field.
2. Ability to understand the qualifications and hiring process for civil service jobs.
3. Ability to develop a systematic approach to finding a job in public-service occupations, and to plan and organize the job search.
4. Ability to gather information needed for preparing job applications.
5. Ability to understand implications of questions on civil service job application forms, and to respond with clarity and directness.
6. Ability to develop understanding and attitudes necessary for taking written examinations for public-service jobs.
7. Ability to select, organize, and present ideas in job interview situations before a qualifications appraisal (oral interview) panel.
8. Ability to make a viable career decision and establish a career direction and goal for continued career development.

CONTENT

INTRODUCTION

This unit is designed:
o to provide an awareness of the basic skills required for employment,
o to impart an understanding of the recruitment and examination process used to fill public-service jobs, and
o to describe procedures, methods, and techniques for applying for a job in the public-service career field.

In presenting this unit, the emphasis will be placed on:

o the understanding of basic job finding and job application techniques,
o the importance of deciding upon an occupational choice,
o the necessity for exploring job requirements in the public-service career field, and
o the importance of planning and organizing the steps to be taken in applying for a job in the public-service field.

1. ## THE PUBLIC SERVICE CAREER FIELD

   As a first step in applying for a job in public-service, attention should be given to understanding the field of public service, and identifying the occupational groups found therein. It is assumed that much of this information has already been covered in prior course work. An earlier publication in this curriculum series, *Orientation to Public Service Occupations,* can be used as a reference in this regard. However, a brief discussion of public-service occupations follows to highlight the wide range of jobs found in public-service occupations.

General Occupational Areas. Public-service employees are at work in occupations representing nearly every kind of job in private industry, as well as some unique to the federal government, such as Postal Clerk, Foreign Service Officer, Immigration Inspector, Border Patrolman, and Internal Revenue Agent. Practically all federal employees are found in jobs under the civil service merit system.

Public service workers are a significant part of the nonagri-cultural work force in every state. Their jobs are found in units of local governments such as counties, municipalities, towns, and school districts. In addition, more than one-fourth of the state and local government work force are employed in state government agencies.

Federal, state, and local employees are at work in offices and laboratories; public schools, colleges, and other educational services and programs; in hospitals, clinics, and libraries; in police and fire protection; in housing and urban renewal; in highway construction and maintenance; in parks and recreation; in public utilities; and in natural resources and conservation.

Public-service workers perform general and financial control activities; work in sewage disposal and water treatment systems; in tax enforcement programs; and in the administration of justice.

Public-service workers collect and distribute the mail; take care of disabled veterans; administer employment, social security, welfare, and health programs; and inspect foods and drugs to see that they are pure.

They check and improve the quality of fruits, vegetables, and other agricultural products; maintain our national parks; forecast the weather; and perform research in the fields of electronics, radio, and radar. They explore the ocean depths and the reaches of space.

All of these activities and functions require workers in such varied occupations as clerk, economist, mathematician, engineer, electrician, forester, educator, pipefitter, and custodian. Clerical, administrative, custodial, and maintenance workers constitute a significant proportion of all employees in many areas of government activity. When we consider the many different governmental agencies, programs, and jurisdictions, and the variety and spread of activities and functions found within them, we can readily see that a diversified work force, with many different levels of education, training, and skill, is required.

The Working Members in Public Service

The thousands of people working in the public-service field come from various socioeconomic levels, and possess many varied skills, aptitudes, talents, abilities, and experiences.

Public-service activities are carried out in offices, establishments, institutions, agencies, schools, and research foundations located in every city, county school district, and State Capitol. The principal offices of most federal agencies are located in Washington, D.C., and their field establishments are scattered throughout the United States and its territories; some even being in foreign countries.

2. THE EMPLOYING AGENCIES

The Civil Service Merit System. With few exceptions, almost all occupations in public service fall under civil service merit systems. Under the merit system, appointments to jobs are made on the basis of ability to do the work - ability demonstrated in competition with other applicants.

All qualified applicants receive consideration for appointment

without regard to any other factor than the results of oral and written examinations. This is a democratic way to fill jobs. It is also a way to make sure that competent persons are hired. Since interested applicants compete with one another for these positions, they are called *competitive positions*. Federal civil service competitive examinations may be taken by all persons who are citizens of the United States, or who owe permanent allegiance to the United States (in the case of residents of American Samoa).

Examinations vary according to the types of positions for which they are held. Some examinations include written tests, others do not. Written tests examine the applicant's ability to do the job applied for, or his ability to learn how to do it.

Applicants are sometimes selected for public-service jobs on the basis of non-written examinations. In non-written examinations, applicants are rated on the basis of the experience and training described in their job application, and any supporting evidence required.

Students should ensure that their applications are filled out carefully and that the information which they provide is clear, complete, and concise. Many disappointed applicants have obtained low eligibility ratings, or have been rated ineligible, because they did not take the time and trouble to read the job announcement carefully and fill out the application forms completely.

State and Local Government Positions. As with the federal civil service, a majority of state and local government public service positions are filled through some type of formal civil service test, and personnel are hired and promoted on the basis of merit.

In some areas, broad groups of employees (such as teachers, firemen, and policemen) have separate civil service coverage which applies only to their specific groups.

Applying for a Job. Almost all types of jobs found in private industry are found in the public-service field.

However, the state, county or city personnel offices, and area offices operated by the U.S.. Civil Service Commission, accept applications for specified types of occupations only when there is a need to fill such positions.

3. CHOOSING A CAREER FIELD

What steps should the student take to help in planning his career choice and development? How well does the student know himself? Does he know about the qualifications needed for occupations in the public service career field? Does he know about the world of work?

These are important considerations for any job. Has the student thought about them?

Gaining Awareness of One's Interests and Abilities. An indi-vidual's interests and abilities go hand-in-hand when considering a career or occupational choice, when planning career development, and when planning the job search. He may have interest, but possess little ability, and would not therefore be able to greatly achieve in a career field. On the other hand, if a student possesses little interest in a career, notwithstanding the fact that he has the ability to perform, he would be ill-advised to choose it for his life's work. *Thus, the student must have both interest in and ability for the career field he chooses.*

Interests. Students should find out what their interests are:

o   What school subjects are most liked?
o   What hobbies, sports, clubs, or part-time jobs are engaged in?
o   Is music an important part of his life? What type?
o   What kinds of reading are done?

A student who may want to think more deeply about his interests may find an *occupational preference test,* or *interest inventory,* helpful in assisting him to relate his interest pattern to the occupations of his choice. A guidance counselor will discuss interests in terms of requirements for various occupational areas. However, students should understand that an interest inventory cannot tell them whether they have the *ability* to perform well in certain occupations.

Abilities. In addition to his interest, one should give serious consideration to his abilities. A good place to start is considering the grades made in some of the school subjects, as in English, languages, social science, history, mathematics, and science, and then listing the strengths and the weaknesses. In addition, the thoughtful person may wish to review his accomplishments in aptitude and achievement tests. These scores may also indicate strong and weak areas of ability. Further-

more, much assistance in this planning can be obtained from discussion of accomplishments and career plans with parents, teachers, and counselors.

It is extremely important to get a clear idea of one's interests and abilities, so there will not be much focus on an occupational field that may be out of reach, or at a level of skill and ability which may under-utilize his capacities and skills. It is equally important that he should choose an occupation that will challenge him, in work that is commensurate with his abilities. This will make his career more rewarding.

Gaining Awareness of Pertinent Personal Factors. As people look at themselves to learn more about their interests and abilities, it is also important to look at other significant personal factors and attributes. Working in the public-service career field generally demands that these individuals must work well with others, either as a member of a team, or of a group performing various activities and functions toward a common goal. It is appropriate to consider how well one gets along with teachers, friends, and neighbors. *Ability to associate well with one's associates is a key to success in whatever endeavor one chooses.*

It is important, and true, to know that a specialized skill may sometimes be no more valuable than a pleasant, cheerful attitude. Students should give some thought to discovering those things they like and dislike, and those biases, prejudices, and inhibitions they may have. On the more positive side, it is well to evaluate how well one can express his feelings, needs, ideas, and strong points.

Importance of Communication Skills. Communication skills are basic to many jobs. Communication is the transfer of information between people; as, for instance, from:
- o   one person to another,
- o   one worker to another,
- o   the businessman to the customer,
- o   the scientist to the layman,
- o   the teacher to the student,
- o   the parent to the child,
- o   the applicant to the personnel interviewer.

Communication calls for trained men and women who can deal with new subject matter, grasp the essentials, and transmit and pass

ideas and facts on to others. No business or endeavor can exist without the use of words. Reading, writing, listening, and speaking have essential roles in applying for a job, and play an important part in the successful performance of almost every endeavor. A job applicant uses language skills to fill out a work application, and to participate in a job interview. It is important to remember that the first impression one makes on a would-be employer may be the most important, and final, impression of all.

The job application and resume should be grammatically correct and correctly punctuated. Use of correct grammar during the oral interview may not get one the job, but the lack of it may make one the least likely candidate for the position.

In many public-service jobs, workers are expected to write memorandums and reports, to develop catalogs, training materials and manuals, to disseminate information, or to talk to groups. If applicants are clear, accurate, and concise in writing and speaking, chances for a good job are improved. *The more easily one can express his ideas, the more self-confidence he is likely to feel.*

4.   **CONSIDERING A PUBLIC SERVICE OCCUPATION**

Selection of one's lifetime occupation is one of the most serious and important steps he ever takes, but, in doing this, one must remember that:

- o   Occupational choice takes a great deal of time.
- o   Occupational choice requires a great amount of knowledge about different careers.
- o   Occupational choice involves much real thought about future goals and expectations.

Selecting the Occupational Group. When thinking about selec-tion of a career in public service, one should become acquainted with the many different occupational groups within the public-service career field; it will be helpful to make mental notes of those occupational categories found to be most attractive.

Since there are so many different occupations within the public service career field, it is perhaps easier to start by selecting from broad occupational groups or families, such as professional, technical, managerial, clerical, or other groups that attract the prospective worker.

Selecting the Occupational Specialty. Once a selection has been made of the occupational groups, proceed to the occupational specialties within those groups, and again find those that are of most interest. When the most attractive occupational specialty has been determined, there is then a need to learn about its educational and experience requirements, and about the responsibilities of the job, in order to determine the necessary qualifications to perform the job. Students will find the curriculum guideline, *Orientation to Public Service Occupations,* and the *Dictionary of Occupational Titles,* a publication of the Manpower Administration, the Department of Labor, of assistance in providing information about skills and requirements of a variety of occupations.

Becoming Aware of Possible Positions. General announcement bulletins tell about job vacancies in many fields. These bulletins should be read carefully to learn:

o   The experience and education which is needed before the application will be accepted,
o   Whether a written test is required,
o   Where the jobs are located, and
o   What the pay is.

The announcement will provide instructions for submitting the job application, and will state the closing date for acceptance of applications. Applications will many times be accepted from students who are taking courses which would permit them to meet the qualifications requirement of the position being sought, and who expect to complete the courses within nine months.

Getting More Information About the Position. The U. S. Civil Service Commission, through its system of area offices located in centers of federal population, announces and conducts examinations; checks applicant's work experience, training, and aptitude; and sends the names of persons who meet the requirements to the agencies seeking new employees.

Each area office also provides, through *its Federal Job Information Center,* a complete one-step information service about federal job opportunities in the immediate area, and in other locations. These Centers provide, at no charge to the applicant, complete information about current job opportunities in any part of the United States, vacancies in *shortage categories* occupations in particular demand by the various federal agencies, opportunities for overseas employment, and employment counseling service. They are especially equipped to answer all inquiries about federal employment opportunities.

Information about current job opportunities and application forms may also be obtained in the local post office, in state, county, or city personnel offices, in public libraries, and school and college placement offices. Recruitment notices are frequently published in newspapers, usually in the classified ad sections.

Closing Dates for Filing Applications. Applications are accepted by the Civil Service Commission or its area office, or by the state, city, county, or local district, as long as the announcement is in an *open* state. In most (but not all) instances, the closing date for filing the application is stated in the announcement. If the closing date is not stated, filing is on an open and continuous basis, and public notice of the closing date is given later. In some cases, the federal government permits persons who cannot apply on time because they are in military service, to apply after the closing date, provided that they apply within 120 days after an honorable, discharge date.

5. ENTRANCE REQUIREMENTS FOR THE POSITION

Reading the Job Announcement. The job announcement should be read carefully. It gives information about the positions to be filled and the required qualifications.

The applicant may prefer to work near his home. If the announcement specifies that the jobs to be filled are in a certain locality and the applicant does not want to work in that location he should not file for the job. On the other hand, he may wish to pay particular attention to more localized employment opportunities in city, county, or state jobs. Federal employment frequently offers many opportunities to live and work away from home.

Unpaid experience or volunteer work (such as in community, cultural, social service, youth, and professional associations) will be given credit on the same basis as that given for paid experience, if it is the type and level acceptable under the announcement. Such experience should be reported in one or more of the experience blocks on the application or personal qualifications statement. The actual time spent in such activities, such as the number of hours per week, should be shown in order to receive proper credit.

The announcements provide specific information about the levels of experience needed. An applicant must be able to show that he has had experience or education at a level comparable in difficulty and responsibility to the specifications listed on the announcement.

Determining Education Requirements. Educational entrance requirements for civil service jobs vary widely. Persons entering into professional occupations are usually required to have highly specialized knowledge in a specified field, as evidenced by completion of a prescribed college course of study, or the equivalent in experience. Typical occupations in this group are physicist, scientist, and engineer.

Entrants into administrative and managerial occupations usually are not required to have knowledge of a specialized field, but rather must indicate by education or responsible job experience, the potential for development. The entrant usually begins at a trainee level and learns the duties of the job after he is hired. Typical jobs in this group are purchasing aide, budget aide, claims examiner, administrative assistant, and personnel aide.

Persons having high school, junior college, or technical school training may apply for such entry-level positions as technician clerical aide, laboratory assistant, supply clerk, educational aide, or Forest Service aide. The entry-level position is usually that of learner or trainee, in which category the duties and specifics of the job are learned, and the skill is improved.

Determining Age Requirements. Although there is no legal discrimination because of age, most individuals are between the ages,of 18 and 65 when hired; the usual minimum is 18, although at the age of 16 high-school graduates may apply for some jobs. If the student is 16 or 17 and out of school, but not a high school graduate, he may be hired only:

o if he has successfully completed a formal training program,
o if he has been out of school at least 3 months, and
o if school authorities sign a form furnished by the hiring agency, agreeing with the individual's preference for work instead of additional schooling.

If the student is still in high school, he may be accepted for work during vacation periods if he is 16, or for part-time work during the school years if he is 16, and meets these conditions:

o His work schedule is set up through agreement with his school,
o His school certifies that he can maintain good standing while working, and
o He remains enrolled in high school.

At the other end of the scale, most public-service agencies will not hire an individual who is over 65 years of age.

Determining Citizenship Requirements. Normally, only American citizens and (American Samoans) may apply for competitive examinations in the Federal Civil Service. Other public-service agencies may require that the applicant be a U. S. citizen or declare his interest to become a U. S. citizen.

Determining Physical Requirements. Candidates for public-service JODS must be physically able to perform the duties of the position, and must be emotionally and mentally stable. Often, a complete physical examination performed by a physician is required before a person can be appointed to a public-service position.

A handicap will not disqualify an applicant if he can perform the work efficiently without being a hazard to himself and others.

The federal government has a special program to encourage the employment of handicapped persons. It recognizes that, in almost every kind of work, there are some positions suitable for the blind, the deaf, and others with serious impairments.

For most positions candidates must have good distant vision in one eye, and be able to read, without strain, printed material the size of typewritten characters. Candidates may use glasses to meet these requirements.

Persons appointed are usually required to hear the conversational voice. A hearing aid may be used.

An amputation of an arm, hand, leg, or foot does not in itself bar a person from federal, state, or local government employment. The criterion is whether the person can handle the job satisfactorily without hazard to himself and others.

However, positions in such occupations as policemen, firefighters, and border patrolman, can be filled only by persons in good physical condition. Physical requirements are normally described in detail in the job announcements.

6. THE JOB APPLICATION

The application is the first step in the examination process, and will constitute the first real contact with the prospective hiring authority. It is, therefore, important that the application be completed carefully and completely.

Detailed requirements of the data required and instructions for filling out and filing the Personal Qualifications Statement, and employment application forms used by the various state, county, city, and municipal civil service boards, are generally attached to and made a part of the application form. Applicants should read these instructions carefully before entering any information on the form.

Assembling the Required Data. The first task in completing the application is to select, arrange, and organize the data needed. To determine needed data, in addition to the requirements listed on the application, the applicant should ask himself, and provide the data to answer, *What parts of my training and experience are relevant to the job goal?*

Prospective applicants may find it helpful to set up a personal file of information needed to complete the application. The file should contain such information as:

o Date of birth,
o Social Security Account Number,
o Names and locations of schools attended,
o Dates of attendance,
o Courses taken,
o Dates of completion,
o Diplomas and/or certificates earned.

In addition, work history should be listed. The work experience should include all data relevant to each job:

o   Name and address of each employer,
o   Beginning and ending dates of employment for each job,
o   Name of supervisor or immediate superior,
o   The job title of the position held,
o   A brief, concise description of the work performed, and
o   The reason for leaving the job.

The personal file should also include the names and addresses of individuals who are willing to provide personal recommendations as to character or skills. Of course, *permission should be obtained from referenced individuals before their names are provided on a work application.*

Filling Out the Application. When sure that he meets requirements listed in the announcement, and that he has gathered all

the information necessary for completing the application, the applicant is ready to fill out the application form.

For some job opportunities, he may have to fill out, at first, only a small card that will be used to admit him to an examination room;

sooner or later, however, he will have to fill out a two or four-page Personal Qualification Statement or application for employment.

The application should be complete and neat. Information should be filled in with typewriter or pen and ink.

Need for Completeness. Every question on the application form or Personal Qualification Statement must be answered fully and accurately. If every question on the form is not answered, the Area Office of the Civil Service Commission, or the state or local civil service board will have to write the applicant to get the missing information. This takes time and causes delay, and could mean loss of employment opportunities.

For many positions, written tests are not required, and applicants are rated solely on their training and experience. Obviously, an applicant cannot get credit for experience or training which he does not claim on his application.

Need for Honesty. It is also important that applicants be completely trutnful in all of their answers. False statements on an application can have serious consequences, and may be grounds for an ineligible rating for employment. In some cases, untruthful answers may even leave one open for prosecution for perjury.

Need for Timeliness. The application should be signed and dated. Instructions in the announcement should be followed as to when and where to send the application. To be considered, applications should be sent to the appropriate office not later than the final filing date.

Importance of the Application. It cannot be stressed too strongly that the application is a part of the examination. It represents the applicant. The information entered on the form will be used to determine that the applicant does or does not meet the entrance requirements, and it may be the basis for arriving at the final rating in the examination. Acceptability for an examination is based on the information provided on the application for that examination, even though the applicant may have prior applications on file.

All applications and supporting documents and attachments become the property of the U. S. Civil Service Commission or other civil service board. None are returned.

7. THE EXAMINATION

The Competitive Examination. If the examination announcement indicated that a written test will be given, a notice will be sent to the applicant telling him when and where to appear for the test. The written test will usually be practical in nature. It will test the candidate's ability to do the job for which he applied, or it will test his ability to learn how to do it.

Studying for the Examination. The student should review the examination announcement carefully to learn as much as possible about the position for which he has applied. The position description will offer some clues as to the subjects which will be tested.

In addition, the examination announcement often has a section called *Scope of Examination* or *Knowledges and Abilities Required.* These sections will help the student in finding out specifically what fields will be tested.

The information in the announcement will also be helpful in choosing suitable study materials. A number of civil service study guides and publications are available at public libraries for self-study in preparing for an examination. Other sources of information are training manuals and publications of a government agency which employs workers in the job for which an application is being made. The applicant may also obtain specific study suggestions by writing or visiting the government department involved. A letter or visit to the agency may also provide specific information as to the exact nature of the position being sought.

Preparing for the Examination. Chances for success on a civil service examination can be increased if common sense is exercised. Nervousness and fatigue are among the most common res-sons why applicants fail to do their best on tests.

Applicants should be reminded to:

o   Begin preparation early.
o   Prepare continuously.
o   Locate the place of the examination.
o   Relax the night before the test.

o   Get up early enough on the day of the examination to allow sufficient time to get to the examination room, with time to spare.
o   Dress comfortably.
o   Leave excess paraphernalia at home.
o   Relax and prepare to listen to the instructions for taking the test.

The Examination Period. Best results are obtained when applicants listen carefully to all instructions, follow directions, and ask questions of the test administrator or monitor when they do not understand what to do.

Civil service examination papers are generally identified by number only. Candidates are assigned numbers for this purpose.

Overall time limits are set for the written test. Candidates should gauge their time carefully in order to complete the test within the time limits. One method is to divide the total time in minutes by the number of questions to get the approximate time one has for each question.

Many capable people are unsuccessful in examinations because they fail to read the questions carefully. It is important that all questions be answered, and that, if time permits, answers be reviewed.

The Unassembled Test. If one applies for a position that does not involve a written test, the rating is based on the experience, education, and training described in the application for work, and any additional information secured by the civil service board, or the Area Office of the U. S. Civil Service Commission, as well as through an oral interview process before a Qualifications Appraisal Panel. Qualifications may also be verified with former employers and supervisors.

In federal civil service announcements that cover several grades or salary levels, the applicant is rated for those he qualifies for, but he is not rated for any grade that pays less than the minimum pay he stated he would accept.

The Oral Interview. The basic purpose of the Qualifications Appraisal Panel is to orally evaluate the candidates1 qualifications, not otherwise measured by a written test, to perform the duties of the position or class for which they are being interviewed, and to establish a ranking for qualified candidates.

The qualifications appraisal or oral interview is generally the final step in the examination process. Its importance is demonstrated by the fact that 40 percent or more of the total score may be assigned to this part of the examination.

In conducting the appraisal, members of the panel are not particularly influenced by the fact that all competitors have passed earlier portions of the examination. Each part of the examination is important in its own right.

An underlying and basic question which concerns each member of the panel is: *If I were the appointing authority, would I hire this individual with reasonable confidence that he could handle the job successfully?*

Preparing for the Interview. Applicants can prepare for the oral interview by thinking about the above question, and having information about his work experience and job-related courses well in mind. Preparation for the interview will prove Us worth. If the student has thought through the manner in which he will present his experience and education, he will be able to bring forth points that will help to establish his qualifications for the position.

Rating the Competitors. The panel will rate competitors on competitive factors, which frequently include the following:

o   *Impression.* Behavior and dress appropriate to the position - tact, poise, neatness and grooming, and maturity.
o   *Presentation.* Communication skills appropriate to the position.
o   *Readiness.* Background and abilities as preparation for this position. Background includes education and experience, work record, self-improvement efforts. Abilities are considered in terms of ability to deal with the practical problems of the job; ability to work effectively with people; ability to adjust to changes in assignment, policies, procedures, etc.

Procedures of Interviewing. Generally, the following proce-dures are followed in interviewing the candidate:
o   Panel members review the candidate's application, to familiarize themselves with the applicant's background, work experience, and educational qualifications.
o   The candidate is brought in and introduced to the panel members.

o   The Chairman of the panel explains the purpose of the interview and asks the candidate to describe the major duties and responsibilities of his present or last job.
o   The panel members ask questions that will encourage the candidate to explain his work experience and qualifications.
o   After the candidate's experience and qualifications have been fully developed in the interview, and panel members have no more questions, the Chairman will ask the applicant if he wishes to add anything that he feels has been overlooked.
o   After the candidate leaves the room, the panel members discuss how well the candidate's qualifications meet the standards for the position, and assign a rating.

Ratings are based exclusively on the information brought out during the interview, or on the candidate's observable behavior in the interview. The ratings are estimates of the candidate's potential success in the position for which he is competing* The ratings are not judgments of his effectiveness in his current job.

8.   THE ELIGIBILITY LIST

Persons who are found to meet the requirements in the announcement are called *eligibles*. The eligible list is made up of those persons who have passed the written and/or the oral examination, and have received a grade.

Scoring for Eligibility. Scoring procedures differ in detail, although the general principles are the same. The papers are usually graded by number, whether or not they are hand-scored or scored by machine. That is, the individual who marks the papers knows only the identification number and not the name of the applicant. Not until all the papers have been graded, will they be matched with names. If other tests, such as for training and experience, or qualifications appraisal (oral interview) ratings have been given, scores will be combined. Different parts of the examination usually have different weights. For example, the written test may count 60 percent of the final grade, and the oral interview rating 40 percent. Veterans may have a certain number of points added to their grades.

Placement on the List. After the final grade has been determined, the names are placed in grade order and an *eligibility list* is established. There are various methods for resolving ties between those who get the same final grade. One of the most common is to place first the name of the person whose

application was received first. Job offers are made from the eligible list in the order the names appear on it. An eligible's chances of getting a job, therefore, depend on his standing on this list, and how fast agencies are filling jobs from the list.

Candidates are notified of their grade and rank order as soon as all of the computations have been made. This is done as rapidly as possible.

Cooperation with the Applicant. Practically all civil service jurisdictions want applicants to understand how their programs operate, and most will permit candidates to review their test papers. Usually this can be done during a specified time after notifications of disqualification or eligibility have been sent.

Filling Jobs from the Eligibility List. When a job is to be filled from the eligibility list, the agency asks the Area Office of the U. S. Civil Service Commission, or the appropriate civil service jurisdiction, for the names of people on the list of eligibles for that job.

Generally, when the civil service office receives this request, it sends to the agency the names of the three people highest on the list. Or, if the job which is to be filled has specialized requirements, the office sends the agency, from the general list, the names of the top three persons who meet those requirements.

The appointing officer makes a choice from among the three people whose names were sent to him. If the elected person accepts the appointment, the names of the others are put back on the list to be considered for future openings.

For most vacancies, the appointing officer has his choice of any one of the top three eligibles on the list. For this reason, it is not automatic that the person whose name is on top of the list always gets the appointment.

9. APPOINTMENT TO A POSITION

Kinds of Appointments. Most appointments in the federal civil service are either career (or permanent), term-career (conditional), or temporary.

A temporary appointment does not ordinarily last more than one year. A temporary worker cannot be promoted, cannot transfer to another job, and is not under the retirement system.

A term appointment is made for work on a specific project that will last more than one year but less than four years. A term employee can be promoted or reassigned to another position within the project for which he is hired. He is usually not under the retirement system. Names of persons who accept temporary or term appointments will remain on the list of eligi-bles from which they were appointed. Thus, they will remain eligible for permanent jobs that are normally filled by career-conditional or career appointments.

A career-conditional appointment leads after three years service to a career appointment. For the first year, the employee serves a probationary period. During this time, he must demonstrate that he can do a satisfactory job, and may be dismissed if he fails to do so. A career-conditional employee has promotion and transfer privileges. After he completes his probation, he cannot be removed except for cause. However, in reduction-in-force (layoff) actions, career-conditional employees are dismissed ahead of career employees.

A career employee serves a probationary period as described above, and has promotion and transfer privileges. After he completes his probation, he is in the last group to be affected in layoffs.

Veterans' Preference. Veterans may be eligible for additional benefits in getting a public-service job. Examination requirements may be waived, and in some circumstances, Vietnam veterans may be hired without competing against other applicants.

Extra examination credits in the form of extra points are added to the veteran's final examination passing score., Disabled veterans or their wives, widowers of certain veterans, and widowed or divorced mothers of some veterans who died in service, or who are totally and permanently disabled by a service-connected disability, usually get 10 extra points. Most other honorably discharged veterans get five points added to the earned scores received on examinations, depending upon length or dates of service.

General Requirements for Appointment. There are certain requirements that must be met before appointment. These requirements are over and above the requirement that one must be able to do the work of the position for which he is being considered.

These requirements include:

o   *Age:* The usual minimum age limit for a federal job is 18 years, but for most jobs, high school graduates may apply at 16, provided that local child-labor laws permit. An

application can be made if the student expects to graduate from high school, or to reach his 18th birthday within six months from the date of filing, but he may not be appointed until he meets the age requirement.

- o *Citizenship:* Candidates must usually be American citizens, or file an intent to become an American citizen.
- o *Physical Condition:* The candidate must be physically, emotionally, and mentally able to perform the duties of the position. As previously stated, a physically handicapped individual is not automatically disqualified. His abilities are assessed to insure that he is not discriminated against because of his handicap.
- o *Residence Requirements:* Residence requirements for many public service jobs are waived. However, appointments to some positions in Washington, D.C., are apportioned by law among the States and territories.

Persons being considered for these positions may be required to submit proof that they meet a one-year residence requirement. When necessary, this proof is requested by the agency considering the candidate for employment.

Security Requirements for Appointment. Before one is hired for the federal civil service, an investigation is made to determine whether the candidate is reliable, trustworthy, of good conduct and character, and loyal to the United States. If the appointment is to a sensitive position where the employee has access to *classified information, a* determination is also made as to whether the individual's employment in the Government service would be clearly consistent with the interests of the national security.

Fingerprints are taken either when one reports for duty or when an investigation has begun. The fingerprints will be sent to the Federal Bureau of Investigation for checking against their records. Applicants must list all convictions other than those for minor traffic violations, or those committed before their 21st birthday and which were finally handled in a juvenile court, or under a youth offender law. Failure to give this information could result in denial or dismissal from federal employment, possible prosecution for perjury, and from employment with other civil service jurisdictions.

10. **ON THE JOB AFTER APPOINTMENT**

Probationary Period. After appointment, the worker will serve a probationary period, generally required by most civil service

jurisdictions, which may last from six months to a year. After the worker has served satisfactorily on probation, he will be notified that he has civil service status with all the related rights.

Pay. Generally, salaries of federal, state, county, and other civil service workers are comparable to those paid by private employers for similar work. Civil service salaries are reviewed frequently, and changes made as needed.

There are several pay plans in the public-service career field. Each grade has a set salary range. In all cases, salaries are listed in the civil-service announcement of position openings. Employees are usually hired at the first rate of grade. If they do their work at an acceptable level of competence, they receive within-grade increases at intervals, until the top rate of the grade is reached.

Hours of Work. The usual work week for federal, state, and local government agencies is 40 hours. Most public service employees work 8 hours a day, five days a week, Monday through Friday. In some cases, the nature of the work may call for a different workweek. This is particularly true in public-safety positions. Required overtime can be compensated for either by pay or by compensatory time-off,

Vacation and Sick Leave. Public-service employees earn both vacation and sick-leave credits. Their earnings of vacation and sick leave may be according to the number of years they have been in service. Sick leave can be used for illness serious enough to keep the employee away from his work and for medical and dental appointments. Unused sick leave can be saved for future use. Vacation leave may be used for vacation purposes, and may be used to supplement sick leave for prolonged illness.

After Appointment to the Job. Even after the applicant has located a job in the public-service career field that he likes and can do well, he may think that there is nothing more to be done.. This is not true. As the new employee gets to know his job better, he will find that he can prepare himself after working hours for more advanced jobs in the federal agency, or in the state, city, county, or local jurisdiction that employs him.

The employee will want to do his job well and prepare for the years ahead by learning more and more about the work of his agency, and becoming more useful on the job. Career development and promotion programs in every agency are designed to make sure that promotions go to the best qualified employees. How fast public-service career employees advance and are promoted depends upon openings in the higher grades, and upon their own ability and effort in getting more education or training to enable them to do better work.

Promotion and Transfer. Agencies consider the qualifications of an employee for promotion as higher grade positions become vacant. Normally, promotional opportunities are limited to those public-service workers who have satisfactorily completed their probationary period. Generally, individuals interested in promotion are required to take a promotional examination to become eligible for advancement. As with open examinations, announcements are made of promotional examinations. *A basic philosophy of public-service agencies is to encourage individuals to take any promotional examination for a position the applicant is qualified for and would like to have.*

Transfers may be made to positions in other agencies. However, in the case of a transfer, the employee has to *find his atn job,* by such means as interviews with officials in those agencies. If he can find a vacant position in another agency, and if the hiring officer is interested, arrangements may be made to transfer him. Federal Job Information Centers and local civil service boards may be able to assist employees in locating vacancies.

Retirement. Public-service employment generally has the advantage of well-established retirement systems. The provisions and amounts differ, depending upon the civil service jurisdiction. Generally, government employees contribute a percentage of their pay to their retirement system. This contribution is deducted directly from the employee's paycheck. A disability provision is also included in most retirement programs.

11. THE FUTURE OF PUBLIC-SERVICE MERIT SYSTEMS

Every American citizen has a continuing interest in the future of the federal government, and of his state, county, municipal, and local jurisdictions. All citizens have an opportunity to participate in the government process, but public-service employees have a special opportunity and responsibility to review and respond to the needs of government.

As a citizen, the student should be aware that it is important to him to protect his interest in government by seeing that only the best qualified persons are selected as public-service employees. The public-service merit system, which insures that all qualified persons will have the opportunity to compete for jobs in the government service, is important in these ways:

o   As citizens, Americans all want public-service jobs to be filled by employees who know how to do their work.
o   As job seekers, Americans all want a fair chance to compete for jobs on an equal footing with other candidates.

The public-service career field offers meaningful work, as well as an opportunity to participate in the operations of government. High standards are set for public-service career people, upon whom the success of the federal, state, and local governments depends. Those students who are inspired to participate in government, and who measure up to these high standards, will find exciting and rewarding careers as government service employees.

STUDENT LEARNING ACTIVITIES

o   Interview public-service workers in various federal, state, city, and local agencies to learn more about how they got their jobs.
o   Obtain and study job announcements and job bulletins issued by federal, state, county, city, or local civil service offices and jurisdictions to learn about current job opportunities and specific job requirements.
o   Set up a personal file of data and information needed to complete an application for work.
o   Obtain and fill out various types of application forms for federal, city, county, and state employment, to develop skills in providing information requested.
o   Obtain position classification descriptions, examination announcements, position listings, bulletins, application forms, and other materials and aids from civil service offices.
o   Obtain copies of civil service study guides and civil service examination aids from a public library. Study the guides, and take sample tests to become acquainted with format of civil service examination questions.
o   Take practice civil service examinations, and score and evaluate your own responses. Place special emphasis on discovering your areas of individual strengths and weaknesses.
o   Actively participate in planned study programs designed to acquaint the student with various entrance requirements, test forms, and practices for filling civil service positions.
o   Participate in a role playing exercise in a qualifications appraisal or oral interview situation, as a member of the qualifications appraisal panel, and/or as a candidate for a civil service job.

23

interview panel. Have students play both the role of the interview panel member (usually 2 or 3) and of the candidate.

o Prepare tapes of different employment interviews and play them for the class to discuss and evaluate.

o Encourage students to use all their senses as qualification panel members to carefully observe what is being communicated by the candidate in the interview.

o Show films on how to apply for a job, for example *Your Job - Applying for It, Job Interview - Whom Would You Hire?*, and *Your Job - Fitting In.*

EVALUATION QUESTIONS
APPLYING FOR CIVIL SERVICE JOBS

1. People are chosen under the civil service system on the basis of:
   A. Interest
   B. Ability
   C. Personal friendship
   D. All of the above

2. A good way to find out one's ability is to take:
   A. An occupational preference test
   B. An interest inventory
   C. An aptitude test
   D. None of the above

3. The best procedure to get a job would be to:
   A. Find out what positions are open, find out more about the positions, then find out your abilities and interests
   B. Apply for a lot of jobs, find out what positions are open, find out about the positions, discover your interests and abilities
   C. Discover your interests and abilities; select your occupational group, then find out about possible positions.
   D. Select your occupational group; apply for many jobs, find out what positions are open.

4. After selecting an occupational group, one should:
   A. Select a specialty
   B. Find out about job vacancies
   C. Get more information about the position
   D. All of the above

5. Persons having high school training may apply for:
   A. Entry level positions such as clerical aide
   B. Manager positions
   C. Professional occupations
   D. None of the above.

6. Information about job opportunities can be found at:
   A. The Federal Job Information Centers
   B. City Personnel Offices
   C. The Post Offices
   D. All of the above

7. These persons are not eligible for civil service jobs:
   A. People between the ages of 18-65 years of age
   B. People who are not citizens of the United States and do not wish to become citizens
   C. Handicapped people who can perform work efficiently

without being a hazard
D. People who are physically able to perform the work required.

8. **Which statement is untrue?**
   A. It is not necessary to put information on applications that can be found on other applications on file.
   B. Work history should include the name and address of each employer and the reason for leaving each job.
   C. Work history should include a brief description of the work performed on each job.
   D. Applicants should list courses taken, dates they were completed, and diplomas earned

9. **Persons who are eligible for most civil service jobs are:**
   A. People over 65 years of age.
   B. Eighteen-year-old high school graduates.
   C. Sixteen-year-olds who have dropped out of high school one month ago.
   D. All of the above.

10. **In preparing for examinations, applicants should:**
    A. Study for the examination.
    B. Locate the place of the examination.
    C. C Leave unnecessary things at home.
    D. All of the above.

11. **On civil service examinations, applicants should not:**
    A. Listen carefully to the instructions.
    B. Leave questions unanswered.
    C. C Follow directions.
    D. Ask the administrator anything.

12. **Which statement about oral interviews is untrue?**
    A. Panel members rate applicants on their behavior and grooming.
    B. Panel members ask questions about the applicant's work experience and background.
    C. It is not necessary to pass the oral interview if the other parts of the examination have been passed.
    D. Applicants should think through how they will present their qualifications so their presentations will be good

13. **Which statement about eligible people for civil service jobs is untrue?**
    A. Papers are graded with the person's name on the paper, then matched to a number.
    B. The eligible list is made up of people who have passed the written and/ or the oral exam.
    C. Papers are graded with a person's number on the paper, then matched to the person's name.
    D. The names are placed in order by the grades received and a list is made in that order

Answer Key

1. B
2. C
3. C
4. D
5. A
6. D
7. B
8. A
9. B
10. D
11. B
12. C
13. A

CIVIL SERVICE EXAMINATIONS
HOW TO TAKE A WRITTEN TEST

I. WHY A TEST?

The State Constitution states that public employees must be hired for jobs on the basis of merit and fitness. The Constitution also says that, for most jobs, merit and fitness must be measured by examination.

In practical terms, hiring employees on the basis of merit and fitness means hiring people who will be able to do the jobs well. State and local governments are no different from private companies. Employers want to hire the best candidates for the jobs.

There are several ways to find good candidates. When private companies hire, they ask candidates about previous work experience, they look at resumes and school records, and they sometimes give tests.

State and local governments also use tests when they hire. All State civil service examinations include one or more tests which are designed to determine how people will perform on certain aspects of the job. Written and oral tests present questions and problems that test candidates for the critical knowledge, skills, and abilities needed on the job. Training and Experience examinations are used to evaluate candidates' possession of the training and experience required to perform the job. Performance tests measure candidates' ability to perform job-related tasks, such as typing or entering computer data.

All civil service examinations are based on the jobs to be filled. Examinations provide a system that is fair and objective. Every candidate for a particular examination answers the same questions or performs the same task and receives a score or scores based on the same factors. This gives all candidates a fair chance to get the jobs, and helps State and local governments to find the people best able to do the jobs. This is the reason the State uses the examination and testing process to fill its state and local civil service jobs.

II. HOW TO FIND OUT ABOUT CIVIL SERVICE EXAMINATIONS

Announcements are published for all State and local (municipal) civil service examinations. You can find out what State civil service examinations are coming up by checking with the State Department of Civil Service. You can find out about local civil service examinations and applications by contacting the municipal civil service agency in the locality of interest. Examination announcements may also be available at local libraries, State Department of Labor Community Service Centers, or placement offices.

III. WHAT A CIVIL SERVICE EXAMINATION ANNOUNCEMENT TELLS YOU

When you pick up a State or local civil service examination announcement, you should read it carefully. The examination announcement will tell you:

- the job titles involved
- the salaries of the titles involved
- the date of the test
- the date by which examination applications must be postmarked
- whether the examination is open competitive or for promotion
- the minimum qualifications (education and/or experience) to take the examination
- the positions (a description of where the jobs exist or are located)
- the duties (a description of the duties of the jobs)
- the subjects of examination
  - whether the test will be written, oral, performance, etc.
  - what subject areas the test will cover
- how to apply
- residency requirements (if any)
- additional information about:
  - admission to the examination
  - religious accommodation
  - reasonable accommodations in testing
  - if multiple examinations are scheduled for the same day
- the processing or application fee (if any) and how the fee may be paid

When you read an examination announcement, you should:

A. Find out what the job is about.

In the examples that follow, we will look at an imaginary examination announcement for Compensation Claims Clerk.

Here are the Positions and Duties statements for the Compensation Claims Clerk.

The Positions: These positions exist in the State Department of Labor and State Insurance Fund.

Duties: As a Compensation Claims Clerk, you would perform responsible clerical work in the development and processing of workers' compensation and disability benefits claims cases. Under supervision, you would organize and determine priority of claims bills; pay certain bills; review claim files; consult appropriate manuals, guidelines, and schedules to determine if treatment is reasonable; verify ratings and compute allowable fees; complete vouchers; and respond to inquiries by doctors, billing offices, and claimants concerning the status of bills. You would also recommend arbitration of disputed fees when appropriate.

This information should help you decide whether you want to be a Compensation Claims Clerk.

To be a Compensation Claims Clerk, you should like to:

- *work with numbers (pay bills; complete vouchers)*
- *read to obtain information (review claim files; consult appropriate manuals, guidelines, and schedules to determine if treatment is reasonable)*
- *keep records and make routine decisions (organize and determine the priority of claims bills; recommend arbitration of disputed fees)*

Think about the kinds of things you like to do. If the duties listed on an examination announcement sound interesting to you, you should read further.

B. Find out whether you qualify for the examination.

Most examinations require a candidate to meet certain minimum qualifications. The minimum qualifications tell you the kind of background you must have in order to take the examination. Because each examination has its own specific minimum qualifications, it is extremely important that you read the minimum qualifications on the examination announcement carefully, to be sure you qualify for the examination.

For example, here are the Minimum Qualifications for Compensation Claims Clerk:

Minimum Qualifications: On or before the date of the written test, candidates must meet the following requirements:

Either possession of a high school diploma or a high school equivalency diploma issued by an appropriate educational authority
or
four years of office, business, industrial, or other work experience which involved public contact; or military experience. Each completed year of high school study (grades 9-12) may be substituted for one year of work experience.

For many civil service examinations, there may be more than one way to meet the minimum qualifications. For example, to qualify for the Compensation Claims Clerk examination, a person could have <u>either</u> a high school diploma <u>or</u> four years of the listed work experience. A person could also have two years of high school study and two years of the listed work experience to qualify.

Education requirements will differ. Some examinations may not require any specific education, while others may require advanced degrees.

C. Find out if there is a residency requirement.

Examinations for some positions may have residency requirements that candidates must meet in order to be eligible to take the test or be appointed.

D. Find out if there is an application fee.

Many examinations require you to pay a non-refundable processing or application fee.

E. **Find out about the subjects of examination.**

For example, here are the Subjects of Examination for Compensation Claims Clerk:

Subjects of Examination: There will be a written test that candidates must pass in order to be considered for appointment. The written test will be designed to test for knowledge, skills and/or abilities in such areas as:

- *Arithmetic computation*
- *Arithmetic reasoning*
- *Understanding and interpreting written material*
- *Office record-keeping*

What does the information above tell you?

First, the examination for Compensation Claim Clerk involves a written test.

Second, the written test for Compensation Claim Clerk will cover four subject areas: arithmetic computation, arithmetic reasoning, understanding and interpreting written material and office record-keeping. (Often, each subject area on an examination announcement will be followed by a paragraph that describes, in more detail, what may be covered in that subject area.)

People hired to be Compensation Claim Clerks must have enough knowledge, skills, and abilities in these subject areas to do the job. These are critical areas of the job. They may not be the only critical areas of the job, but they are the only ones that will be covered by the written test for Compensation Claim Clerk.

Once you determine that you are interested in the job, meet the minimum qualifications for the job, and wish to take the examination for the job, you should apply for the examination.

IV. **HOW TO APPLY FOR THE EXAMINATION**

The examination announcement will tell you, under How To Apply, the examination application form required, where to get it, and how to file it. Once you have the correct form, fill it out carefully, accurately, completely, and neatly. Read all parts and fill out all of those that apply to you.

The information you provide must show that you meet the minimum qualifications required to take the test. Therefore, it is important that you answer all questions and provide clear and complete information about your relevant education and experience.

Reasonable accommodations in testing can be arranged for people with disabilities. If you need reasonable accommodations to take the test, you should indicate this on our application for the examination. You must also directly contact the civil service agency that announced the examination (the Department of Civil Service for State examinations or the local civil service agency for local examinations) to describe the accommodations

22

- Observe interviews during role playing exercises to evaluate effectiveness of candidate's responses. Be prepared to discuss techniques used to overcome problems that develop.
- Listen to examples of interviews on tape, and be prepared to rate the candidate exclusively on information brought out during the interview, or on the candidate's observable behavior during the interview.
- Talk to your school guidance counselor or psychologist about your career choice.
- Consult the Dictionary of Occupational Titles and the Occupational Outlook Handbook about skills and the requirements of a variety of occupations in the public-service field.
- View films on how to apply for jobs, for example *Your Job - Applying for It, Job Interview - Whom Would You Hire?,* and *Your Job - Fitting In.*

TEACHER MANAGEMENT ACTIVITIES

- Plan on utilizing role playing exercises to acquaint students with communication skills in qualifications appraisal or oral interview situations.
- Arrange to have representatives of federal, state, county, and city civil service agencies and government offices visit the class and discuss career opportunities and application procedures.
- Provide opportunities for the school counselor or psychologist to discuss various considerations in arriving at occupational or career choice.
- Encourage students to adopt an exploratory attitude aimed at sharpening their awareness of job opportunities in the public-service career field.
- Collect samples of practice civil service test materials and publications and brochures available through civil service commissions and boards to discuss and review with students;
- Conduct simulated civil service tests under actual, timed testing conditions to provide students with test taking experiences.
- Have students score or evaluate their own responses and identify their individual strengths and weaknesses in basic verbal and math areas.
- Encourage students needing to improve their basic skills to enroll in special remedial courses or to perform self study/in order to increase their effectiveness in taking written civil service examinations.

- Obtain copies of various civil service bulletins and announcements. Discuss various job specifications in terms of general and specific education, experience, and hiring requirements.
- Utilize role playing exercises to acquaint students with the purposes and procedures of the qualifications appraisal or oral

you need. You will be required to produce documentation to prove that you are eligible for reasonable accommodations in testing.

Alternate test date arrangements are also available for Sabbath observers, persons on active military duty, and persons taking examinations for more than one civil service jurisdiction on the same date.

War-time disabled veterans, war-time veterans, and persons on full-time active duty (other than for training) are eligible to have extra credits added to their examination score, if they pass. In most instances, these extra credits can be used only once for any permanent government appointment in the State. If you want to have the extra credits added to your examination score, you must answer the appropriate questions on the application form. You will be required to produce documentation, such as discharge papers, to prove that you are eligible for veterans credits.

On the application form, there is a place to sign a statement which affirms that all the information you have given is accurate. This is your legal affirmation that the statements on our application are true.

You will be required to pay an application fee to take most examinations. Information on the amount of the fee and how it can be paid will be found on the announcement. If some applicants are eligible to have the required fee waived, the announcement will explain the requirements for a waiver.

Follow the instructions for completing your application and submit the application by the date shown on the announcement. It is advisable to keep a photocopy of your application along with the examination announcement for your records.

Mark the test date on your calendar!

V. YOUR ADMISSION NOTICE

Approximately one week before the test date, you will receive an admission notice for the test. The admission notice will tell you the date, time, and place of the test, and will list the examination numbers of the tests you are scheduled to take on that test date. You will have to present this notice at the test center, so be sure to save it. The admission notice will also tell you if you should bring anything to the test, such as sharpened No. 2 pencils, a calculator, or a quiet lunch.

The admission notice will also tell you that you must bring identification to the test center. The identification must show your name, signature, and photograph. A driver's license or a picture ID will do. If you have not received an admission notice by the Wednesday before the test date, or if you lose your admission notice, you should call the State or municipal civil service department that announced the examination to find out what you should do.

VI. HOW TO PREPARE FOR THE TEST

In most cases, you will have some time between when you apply for an examination and the date of the test. You can use this time to prepare yourself for taking the test so that you can do your best on the test date. The next sections of this booklet will give you some general test-taking guidelines that should be helpful.

The following information applies to civil service multiple-choice tests, although some of the information may be helpful in preparing for an oral test or a performance test as well.

A. Preparing For the Test

Most State civil service examinations include a multiple-choice test. The examination announcement will list the Subjects of Examination that the test will cover. Use this information to help prepare for the test.

For example, the Subjects of Examination on the examination announcement for the Compensation Claims Clerk listed four subject areas:

- Arithmetic computation
- Arithmetic reasoning
- Understanding and interpreting written material
- Office record-keeping

Often, the name of the subject area will give you a good idea about what will be covered in that area. For example, "Arithmetic computation" would cover simple arithmetic operations like addition, subtraction, multiplication, division, percents, and averages.

Usually, the announcement contains (or indicates where you can get) an expanded description of what will be covered in a subject area. For example, the expanded description for "Arithmetic reasoning" reads: *"These questions test your ability to solve arithmetic problems presented in sentence or short paragraph form. You must read the problem, understand the situation presented, decide what must be done to solve it, and apply the appropriate arithmetic operation(s), in the appropriate order, to determine the correct answer. Knowledge of addition, subtraction, multiplication, and division will be necessary. Questions may also involve the use of percents, decimals, and fractions."*

There are certain words that often appear in the names and expanded descriptions of the subject areas of an examination:

- principles, practices, procedures, methods, techniques
- understanding, interpreting, applying, reasoning, solving

The first group of words generally indicates that you will be asked about your knowledge of the principles, practices, procedures, methods, and/or techniques of the particular subject area.

The second group of words generally indicates that you will be tested for the skill or ability to understand, interpret, apply, reason, and/or solve problems and/or information in the particular subject area.

B. **Preparing for a Test of Knowledge**

To prepare for a test of knowledge, you can:

- buy an NLC Test Prep Passbook®
- read books, magazines, manuals, or other printed material on the subject area
- ask people who know a lot about the subject for information
- rely on your own background (think about your experience in the subject area)

C. **Preparing for a Test of Skill or Ability**

Preparing for a test of skill or ability may be a bit more difficult. If you want to improve your skill or ability in a certain area, your best preparation is practice.

Skills like keyboarding are easy to practice – you sit down at a keyboard and type. To improve other skills, you may need to be more creative.

For example, if you are going to be tested on your skill in preparing written material, you can try writing a few paragraphs about an event you attended or a project you completed. Then ask others to read what you wrote. Ask them to tell you whether your paragraphs were clear to them. Ask if there were parts that needed to be rewritten. Get suggestions for improving your grammar, punctuation, and sentence structure from writers or writing teachers. There are plenty of textbooks that contain the rules of good writing, grammar, and punctuation. Learn the rules; then practice them. Then go back and try again.

Books can help you improve our arithmetic skills. Arithmetic computation involves skill in correctly performing computations such as addition, subtraction, multiplication, division, percentages, fractions, etc. Arithmetic reasoning involves skill in understanding and solving problems that use arithmetic. Here is an example of such a problem:

A company owned six trucks and three vans in March. It sold two trucks in April and two vans in May. The company did not buy any trucks or vans until July. How many vehicles did the company have in June?

The answer is 5. (6 trucks + 3 vans = 9 vehicles owned in March; 2 trucks in April + 2 vans in May = 4 vehicles sold; 9 vehicles owned in March minus 4 vehicles sold in April and May = 5 vehicles left in June.)

Arithmetic computation and arithmetic reasoning problems can be found in schoolbooks or library books. You can practice solving the problems until you are more comfortable with them.

In general, the more you learn about a job, the better you can prepare for the examination. Learn to use the examination announcement as a guide – the whole announcement, not just the Subjects of Examination portion. If you decide you need to study, start early. You will probably remember more if you study when you are relaxed than if you wait until the night before the examination.

D. **Computer-Administered Multiple-Choice Tests**

Although most civil service multiple-choice tests are administered in paper and pencil form, some are administered on personal computers at central test locations. Candidates read and answer a computer-administered multiple-choice test directly on a personal computer at a test center. The number of computer-administered tests is expected to grow as personal computers become more available and as computer technology advances. The examination announcement will indicate whether a test is to be computer-administered.

VII. **GENERAL TEST-TAKING GUIDELINES**

A. **Read all test directions and instructions carefully.** Make sure that you carefully read and follow all directions and any special instructions for the test. If sample questions are provided, do them for practice. Make sure you understand the directions and instructions before you start to answer the questions.

B. **Make sure you are answering the correct test questions in the correct test booklets.** The particular test you are taking may involve skipping some questions in the test booklet or may involve answering questions in more than one test booklet. You are responsible for making sure you get the right test booklet for your particular test and for determining which questions you are to answer. Refer to your test materials for information on which test booklets and questions you are to answer.

C. **Make sure the choice you mark on your answer sheet matches the question you are answering in the test booklet.** Most written multiple-choice tests are scanned and scored by machine. You will not get credit for choices you mark in the wrong place on the answer sheet. Check your work to make sure that the number of the question you are answering in the test booklet matches the choice you are marking on your answer sheet.

D. **Make sure you record all your answers on the answer sheet.** Only the answers you mark on your answer sheet will be counted toward your score.

E. **Make sure you fill in the circles for your choices, completely and carefully.** Avoid making stray pencil marks on your answer sheet. The scanning machine may interpret these marks to be your answers.

F. **Budget your time wisely.** Take note of the test time allowance and of the starting and stopping times. Look at the whole test first, then decide how much time to allow yourself for each part. You get just as much credit for an easy question as for a hard one. You may want to answer the easy questions first. Do not take too much time trying to answer the difficult questions. Jot down the number of the difficult questions and then come back to them later if you have time. (If you do skip a question in the test booklet, make sure you skip that answer on your answer sheet as well.) Keep track of the time as you go through the test. Know how much time you have and how many questions you have left to do. If some parts of your test are separately timed, work as rapidly as you can but stay calm and pay attention to the time limit.

G. **Read each question carefully.** Make sure you read what is actually printed in the test booklet. The questions are designed to test your knowledge, skills, or abilities in a subject area. They are not meant to trick you or to be deceptive. Read each question carefully, follow the directions given, and answer each question based on the information given and on the actual question asked. After you read the question carefully, read each choice carefully. Make sure that you understand each choice before you decide which one is best. Pick the one choice that best answers the question given. Do not jump to conclusions. Be thorough and think about all the choices. If you do not read each choice carefully, you could easily miss the best one.

H. **Be alert to key words that you must consider to answer the question correctly.** Key words establish a condition that only the correct answer meets. Words like *best*, *greatest*, *always*, or *most* are examples of key words. If a question asks you to identify the *best* choice among four given, it may be that each of the four choices is a possible answer, but only one of the four choices is the best answer. To answer this type of question correctly, you must carefully read and compare all the choices given.

Here are some examples of questions which contain key words:

1. Of the following foods, which one provides the most vitamin C in a one-cup serving?
   A. Grapefruit juice
   B. Sliced peaches
   C. Mashed potatoes
   C. Chopped broccoli

Answer: This question asks which of the foods listed provides the **most** vitamin C in a one-cup serving. The key word in this question is **most**. All of the foods mentioned in the choices contain some vitamin C. Many people know that citrus fruits, like oranges, lemons, and grapefruits, are good sources of vitamin C. That makes choice A look attractive. But one cup of broccoli actually contains more vitamin C than one cup of grapefruit juice. Choice D is the best answer. To answer this question correctly, you must read all four choices carefully before you can determine the best answer.

2. Of the following, which one is generally the best way to repair a Compton machine that will not start?
   A. Replace the entire engine
   B. Replace the ignition wires
   C. Clean the carburetor
   D. Clean the valves

Answer: This question asks which one of the choices listed is generally the best way to repair a Compton machine that will not start. The key words in this question are **generally** and **best**. Assume that in 99 out of 100 cases, the best way to repair a Compton machine that will not start is to replace the ignition wires. Then choice B, replace the ignition wires, is **generally** the **best** way to do the repair. Choice B is the correct answer to this question.

Questions that use words like *generally* and *usually* are looking for the rule, not the exception. Other key words of this type are *common*, *likely*, *more*, *often*, *primarily*, *probably*, *typically*, and *usually*. When you see these words in a question, look for the choice that would be correct most of the time. Do not choose the one that would be correct only some of the time or on rare occasions.

Be alert to questions that use words like *disadvantage*, *except*, *least*, and *not*. If the question asks about a *disadvantage*, be sure not to choose an advantage as your answer. Words that begin with *non-* or *un-* are ways of saying *not*.

3. If grease in a pan catches fire, it is unwise to do which one of the following?
    A. Cover the pan with a lid
    B. Pour water on the fire

Answer: This question asks you to identify which action is unwise to do if grease in a pan catches fire. The key word in this question is **unwise**. This word should alert you that the question is looking for what you should **not** do, rather than what you should do if grease in a pan catches fire. Choice A, covering the pan with a lid, would smother the fire by cutting off the oxygen it needs to burn. Choice A is what you should do if grease in a pan catches fire. However, since this question asks what is **unwise** to do, choice A is the wrong answer to this question. Choice B, pouring water on the fire, would cause the grease and fire in the pan to spatter because water and grease do not mix. This could cause injury or make the fire spread. So, it is *unwise* to pour water on the fire. Therefore, Choice B is the correct answer to this question.

4. If an alarm goes off in a mechanical room and the situation appears to be a threat to health or safety, what should you do first?
    A. Turn off the power.
    B. Call your supervisor.
    C. Call the security staff.
    D. Have people leave the area.

Answer: This question asks what you should do first if an alarm goes off in a mechanical room. The key word in this question is **first**. When a question uses the word *first*, consider the choices in the order in which they should be done. For the question above, all four choices list actions that should be taken. The important thing to know is which to do first in the situation. Since the situation could be life-threatening or could result in injury, the first thing to do is to have people leave the area. This allows people to remain safe while the reason for the alarm is determined and the situation is fixed. Choice D is the first thing to do. If the situation were **not** life-threatening, choice A, turning off the power, might be the first thing to do.

When you see a question like this, make sure you understand the question and the situation thoroughly. When you think you have decided the right order for the actions, mark down the choice that you think is the first action to take in the situation. That way, you think about the whole series of possible actions to take, not just one action by itself, and you are more likely to choose the correct answer.

I. **Break large problems into more manageable parts and analyze each part.** A very large or complex problem may make more sense if you break it down and look at it one part at a time. Make diagrams or notes on your scrap paper to help you understand each of the separate parts, and how those parts collectively make up the whole problem. Sometimes you can work backwards from the answer to see which answer best fits the problem. Try each answer, in turn, to find the one that works best.

J. **Use a process of elimination, if you are not sure about the answer to a question.** Most multiple-choice questions give you four possible choices. You may not be sure of the answer, but you may see right away that one or two of the choices are not correct. If this is the case, immediately eliminate the choices you know are not correct. Then, just think about the others. Pick the best of the choices that remain. Even if one choice seems only a little better than the others, pick that one. If you can eliminate one or more of the choices and make an educated guess about the choices that remain, your chances of success are better than if you make a completely wild guess.

K. **Guess, if you do not know the answer to a question.** If you do not answer a question, you will not get credit for it. If you guess correctly, you will get credit. Therefore, if you are not sure of an answer, you should still try to answer the question.

VIII. ON THE DAY BEFORE THE TEST

On the day before the test, you should prepare just as you would for any other important appointment. Know where you are going and explore your options for getting there. Check bus or subway connections or get information about where to park ahead of time.

Prepare what you should take with you to the test. Review the examination announcement and your admission notice to identify everything you need to bring with you to the test. [For example, sharpened No. 2 pencils, a driver's license or picture ID, your admission notice, a watch (to time yourself if you cannot see a clock), a quiet hand-held calculator without keyboard (if allowed), or other required materials.] Since many tests last three or more hours, you may want to bring a quiet lunch or a snack and beverage with you.

Get plenty of rest the night before the test and allow yourself enough time in the morning so that you do not have to rush. Being rested and having a clear head on the day of the test may help as much as any last minute review.

Be aware that you may **not** bring cellular phones, beepers, headphones, or other similar communication devices to the test center. The use of such devices at the test center is strictly prohibited and can result in your disqualification.

Be aware that smoking is **not** allowed at the test center or on the test center grounds.

IX. ON THE TEST DAY

When you leave for the test, allow yourself extra time to find parking, to locate the room where you will be taking the test, and to get yourself settled. Be aware, however, that you will not be allowed into the test center until one-half hour before your reporting time.

A. Test Monitors

There will be test monitors in the building and room where you take the test. The monitors will assure that the tests you are taking are administered fairly to all candidates. On your desk or table you should find the answer sheet for your test, with directions on how to complete it, and a copy of the Candidate Directions. Take the time to look these over while you wait for the test to begin.

B. The Candidate Directions

Be sure to read the Candidate Directions carefully. The Candidate Directions include information specific to our test, such as the time allowance for the test, what test booklets and test questions you are to answer, and how the questions will be valued. (Unless the Candidate Directions state otherwise, all questions will be valued the same.) The Candidate Directions will contain explicit information about which questions you are to answer. For some tests, you may not have to answer every question in every test booklet, but you may have to answer some questions in several test booklets. It is important that you read the Candidate Directions **very** carefully. You are responsible for determining which questions you are to answer. **The monitor cannot help you to determine which questions you are to answer.** That part is up to you.

C. Beginning the Test

The monitor will begin the testing process by announcing what test(s) are being given in your test room. Listen to the monitor carefully and make sure you are in the correct test room. The monitor will then verify your identification and have you sign your admission notice. After the identification and admission process is complete, the monitor may give you some oral instructions, will distribute the test booklets, and will tell you when you may begin the test.

D. During the Test

Although test monitors cannot answer questions about the test itself, they can assist you if something goes wrong, if there is a defect in your test booklet, or if you have to leave the room for a legitimate purpose. Just raise your hand and a monitor will assist you. If someone or something is distracting you, bring it to the monitor's attention. Do not look at the work of other people in the room or you may be disqualified.

E. Ending the Test

Before you leave the test room, you must return all the test materials you were given, including scrap paper. Raise your hand when you are finished with the test.

A monitor will come to your desk to check and collect all your test materials before dismissing you from the test.

X. A FINAL WORD

Keep a positive attitude. Your attitude can affect how well you do on a test. If you are aware of what to expect on test day, read all the test materials carefully, listen to the monitors, follow the directions given, and keep a positive attitude, you will do your best.

Good Luck!

HOW TO TAKE A TEST

I. YOU MUST PASS AN EXAMINATION

A. WHAT EVERY CANDIDATE SHOULD KNOW

Examination applicants often ask us for help in preparing for the written test. What can I study in advance? What kinds of questions will be asked? How will the test be given? How will the papers be graded?

As an applicant for a civil service examination, you may be wondering about some of these things. Our purpose here is to suggest effective methods of advance study and to describe civil service examinations.

Your chances for success on this examination can be increased if you know how to prepare. Those "pre-examination jitters" can be reduced if you know what to expect. You can even experience an adventure in good citizenship if you know why civil service exams are given.

B. WHY ARE CIVIL SERVICE EXAMINATIONS GIVEN?

Civil service examinations are important to you in two ways. As a citizen, you want public jobs filled by employees who know how to do their work. As a job seeker, you want a fair chance to compete for that job on an equal footing with other candidates. The best-known means of accomplishing this two-fold goal is the competitive examination.

Exams are widely publicized throughout the nation. They may be administered for jobs in federal, state, city, municipal, town or village governments or agencies.

Any citizen may apply, with some limitations, such as the age or residence of applicants. Your experience and education may be reviewed to see whether you meet the requirements for the particular examination. When these requirements exist, they are reasonable and applied consistently to all applicants. Thus, a competitive examination may cause you some uneasiness now, but it is your privilege and safeguard.

C. HOW ARE CIVIL SERVICE EXAMS DEVELOPED?

Examinations are carefully written by trained technicians who are specialists in the field known as "psychological measurement," in consultation with recognized authorities in the field of work that the test will cover. These experts recommend the subject matter areas or skills to be tested; only those knowledges or skills important to your success on the job are included. The most reliable books and source materials available are used as references. Together, the experts and technicians judge the difficulty level of the questions.

Test technicians know how to phrase questions so that the problem is clearly stated. Their ethics do not permit "trick" or "catch" questions. Questions may have been tried out on sample groups, or subjected to statistical analysis, to determine their usefulness.

Written tests are often used in combination with performance tests, ratings of training and experience, and oral interviews. All of these measures combine to form the best-known means of finding the right person for the right job.

II. HOW TO PASS THE WRITTEN TEST

A. NATURE OF THE EXAMINATION

To prepare intelligently for civil service examinations, you should know how they differ from school examinations you have taken. In school you were assigned certain definite pages to read or subjects to cover. The examination questions were quite detailed and usually emphasized memory. Civil service exams, on the other hand, try to discover your present ability to perform the duties of a position, plus your potentiality to learn these duties. In other words, a civil service exam attempts to predict how successful you will be. Questions cover such a broad area that they cannot be as minute and detailed as school exam questions.

In the public service similar kinds of work, or positions, are grouped together in one "class." This process is known as *position-classification*. All the positions in a class are paid according to the salary range for that class. One class title covers all of these positions, and they are all tested by the same examination.

B. FOUR BASIC STEPS

1) Study the announcement

How, then, can you know what subjects to study? Our best answer is: "Learn as much as possible about the class of positions for which you've applied." The exam will test the knowledge, skills and abilities needed to do the work.

Your most valuable source of information about the position you want is the official exam announcement. This announcement lists the training and experience qualifications. Check these standards and apply only if you come reasonably close to meeting them.

The brief description of the position in the examination announcement offers some clues to the subjects which will be tested. Think about the job itself. Review the duties in your mind. Can you perform them, or are there some in which you are rusty? Fill in the blank spots in your preparation.

Many jurisdictions preview the written test in the exam announcement by including a section called "Knowledge and Abilities Required," "Scope of the Examination," or some similar heading. Here you will find out specifically what fields will be tested.

2) Review your own background

Once you learn in general what the position is all about, and what you need to know to do the work, ask yourself which subjects you already know fairly well and which need improvement. You may wonder whether to concentrate on improving your strong areas or on building some background in your fields of weakness. When the announcement has specified "some knowledge" or "considerable knowledge," or has used adjectives like "beginning principles of…" or "advanced … methods," you can get a clue as to the number and difficulty of questions to be asked in any given field. More questions, and hence broader coverage, would be included for those subjects which are more important in the work. Now weigh your strengths and weaknesses against the job requirements and prepare accordingly.

3) Determine the level of the position

Another way to tell how intensively you should prepare is to understand the level of the job for which you are applying. Is it the entering level? In other words, is this the position in which beginners in a field of work are hired? Or is it an intermediate or advanced level? Sometimes this is indicated by such words as "Junior" or "Senior" in the class title. Other jurisdictions use Roman numerals to designate the level – Clerk I, Clerk II, for example. The word "Supervisor" sometimes appears in the title. If the level is not indicated by the title, check the description of duties. Will you be working under very close supervision, or will you have responsibility for independent decisions in this work?

4) Choose appropriate study materials

Now that you know the subjects to be examined and the relative amount of each subject to be covered, you can choose suitable study materials. For beginning level jobs, or even advanced ones, if you have a pronounced weakness in some aspect of your training, read a modern, standard textbook in that field. Be sure it is up to date and has general coverage. Such books are normally available at your library, and the librarian will be glad to help you locate one. For entry-level positions, questions of appropriate difficulty are chosen – neither highly advanced questions, nor those too simple. Such questions require careful thought but not advanced training.

If the position for which you are applying is technical or advanced, you will read more advanced, specialized material. If you are already familiar with the basic principles of your field, elementary textbooks would waste your time. Concentrate on advanced textbooks and technical periodicals. Think through the concepts and review difficult problems in your field.

These are all general sources. You can get more ideas on your own initiative, following these leads. For example, training manuals and publications of the government agency which employs workers in your field can be useful, particularly for technical and professional positions. A letter or visit to the government department involved may result in more specific study suggestions, and certainly will provide you with a more definite idea of the exact nature of the position you are seeking.

III. KINDS OF TESTS

Tests are used for purposes other than measuring knowledge and ability to perform specified duties. For some positions, it is equally important to test ability to make adjustments to new situations or to profit from training. In others, basic mental abilities not dependent on information are essential. Questions which test these things may not appear as pertinent to the duties of the position as those which test for knowledge and information. Yet they are often highly important parts of a fair examination. For very general questions, it is almost impossible to help you direct your study efforts. What we can do is to point out some of the more common of these general abilities needed in public service positions and describe some typical questions.

1) General information

Broad, general information has been found useful for predicting job success in some kinds of work. This is tested in a variety of ways, from vocabulary lists to questions about current events. Basic background in some field of work, such as sociology or economics, may be sampled in a group of questions. Often these are principles which have become familiar to most persons through exposure rather than through formal training. It is difficult to advise you how to study for these questions; being alert to the world around you is our best suggestion.

2) Verbal ability

An example of an ability needed in many positions is verbal or language ability. Verbal ability is, in brief, the ability to use and understand words. Vocabulary and grammar tests are typical measures of this ability. Reading comprehension or paragraph interpretation questions are common in many kinds of civil service tests. You are given a paragraph of written material and asked to find its central meaning.

3) Numerical ability

Number skills can be tested by the familiar arithmetic problem, by checking paired lists of numbers to see which are alike and which are different, or by interpreting charts and graphs. In the latter test, a graph may be printed in the test booklet which you are asked to use as the basis for answering questions.

4) Observation

A popular test for law-enforcement positions is the observation test. A picture is shown to you for several minutes, then taken away. Questions about the picture test your ability to observe both details and larger elements.

5) Following directions

In many positions in the public service, the employee must be able to carry out written instructions dependably and accurately. You may be given a chart with several columns, each column listing a variety of information. The questions require you to carry out directions involving the information given in the chart.

6) Skills and aptitudes

Performance tests effectively measure some manual skills and aptitudes. When the skill is one in which you are trained, such as typing or shorthand, you can practice. These tests are often very much like those given in business school or high school courses. For many of the other skills and aptitudes, however, no short-time preparation can be made. Skills and abilities natural to you or that you have developed throughout your lifetime are being tested.

Many of the general questions just described provide all the data needed to answer the questions and ask you to use your reasoning ability to find the answers. Your best preparation for these tests, as well as for tests of facts and ideas, is to be at your physical and mental best. You, no doubt, have your own methods of getting into an exam-taking mood and keeping "in shape." The next section lists some ideas on this subject.

IV. KINDS OF QUESTIONS

Only rarely is the "essay" question, which you answer in narrative form, used in civil service tests. Civil service tests are usually of the short-answer type. Full instructions for answering these questions will be given to you at the examination. But in case this is your first experience with short-answer questions and separate answer sheets, here is what you need to know:

1) Multiple-choice Questions

Most popular of the short-answer questions is the "multiple choice" or "best answer" question. It can be used, for example, to test for factual knowledge, ability to solve problems or judgment in meeting situations found at work.

A multiple-choice question is normally one of three types—

- It can begin with an incomplete statement followed by several possible endings. You are to find the one ending which *best* completes the statement, although some of the others may not be entirely wrong.
- It can also be a complete statement in the form of a question which is answered by choosing one of the statements listed.
- It can be in the form of a problem – again you select the best answer.

Here is an example of a multiple-choice question with a discussion which should give you some clues as to the method for choosing the right answer:

When an employee has a complaint about his assignment, the action which will *best* help him overcome his difficulty is to

- A. discuss his difficulty with his coworkers
- B. take the problem to the head of the organization
- C. take the problem to the person who gave him the assignment
- D. say nothing to anyone about his complaint

In answering this question, you should study each of the choices to find which is best. Consider choice "A" – Certainly an employee may discuss his complaint with fellow employees, but no change or improvement can result, and the complaint remains unresolved. Choice "B" is a poor choice since the head of the organization probably does not know what assignment you have been given, and taking your problem to him is known as "going over the head" of the supervisor. The supervisor, or person who made the assignment, is the person who can clarify it or correct any injustice. Choice "C" is, therefore, correct. To say nothing, as in choice "D," is unwise. Supervisors have and interest in knowing the problems employees are facing, and the employee is seeking a solution to his problem.

2) True/False Questions

The "true/false" or "right/wrong" form of question is sometimes used. Here a complete statement is given. Your job is to decide whether the statement is right or wrong.

SAMPLE: A roaming cell-phone call to a nearby city costs less than a non-roaming call to a distant city.

This statement is wrong, or false, since roaming calls are more expensive.

This is not a complete list of all possible question forms, although most of the others are variations of these common types. You will always get complete directions for answering questions. Be sure you understand *how* to mark your answers – ask questions until you do.

V. RECORDING YOUR ANSWERS

Computer terminals are used more and more today for many different kinds of exams.

For an examination with very few applicants, you may be told to record your answers in the test booklet itself. Separate answer sheets are much more common. If this separate answer sheet is to be scored by machine – and this is often the case – it is highly important that you mark your answers correctly in order to get credit.

An electronic scoring machine is often used in civil service offices because of the speed with which papers can be scored. Machine-scored answer sheets must be marked with a pencil, which will be given to you. This pencil has a high graphite content which responds to the electronic scoring machine. As a matter of fact, stray dots may register as answers, so do not let your pencil rest on the answer sheet while you are pondering the correct answer. Also, if your pencil lead breaks or is otherwise defective, ask for another.

Since the answer sheet will be dropped in a slot in the scoring machine, be careful not to bend the corners or get the paper crumpled.

The answer sheet normally has five vertical columns of numbers, with 30 numbers to a column. These numbers correspond to the question numbers in your test booklet. After each number, going across the page are four or five pairs of dotted lines. These short dotted lines have small letters or numbers above them. The first two pairs may also have a "T" or "F" above the letters. This indicates that the first two pairs only are to be used if the questions are of the true-false type. If the questions are multiple choice, disregard the "T" and "F" and pay attention only to the small letters or numbers.

Answer your questions in the manner of the sample that follows:

32. The largest city in the United States is
    A. Washington, D.C.
    B. New York City
    C. Chicago
    D. Detroit
    E. San Francisco

1) Choose the answer you think is best. (New York City is the largest, so "B" is correct.)
2) Find the row of dotted lines numbered the same as the question you are answering. (Find row number 32)
3) Find the pair of dotted lines corresponding to the answer. (Find the pair of lines under the mark "B.")
4) Make a solid black mark between the dotted lines.

VI. BEFORE THE TEST

Common sense will help you find procedures to follow to get ready for an examination. Too many of us, however, overlook these sensible measures. Indeed, nervousness and fatigue have been found to be the most serious reasons why applicants fail to do their best on civil service tests. Here is a list of reminders:

- Begin your preparation early – Don't wait until the last minute to go scurrying around for books and materials or to find out what the position is all about.
- Prepare continuously – An hour a night for a week is better than an all-night cram session. This has been definitely established. What is more, a night a week for a month will return better dividends than crowding your study into a shorter period of time.
- Locate the place of the exam – You have been sent a notice telling you when and where to report for the examination. If the location is in a different town or otherwise unfamiliar to you, it would be well to inquire the best route and learn something about the building.
- Relax the night before the test – Allow your mind to rest. Do not study at all that night. Plan some mild recreation or diversion; then go to bed early and get a good night's sleep.
- Get up early enough to make a leisurely trip to the place for the test – This way unforeseen events, traffic snarls, unfamiliar buildings, etc. will not upset you.
- Dress comfortably – A written test is not a fashion show. You will be known by number and not by name, so wear something comfortable.
- Leave excess paraphernalia at home – Shopping bags and odd bundles will get in your way. You need bring only the items mentioned in the official notice you received; usually everything you need is provided. Do not bring reference books to the exam. They will only confuse those last minutes and be taken away from you when in the test room.
- Arrive somewhat ahead of time – If because of transportation schedules you must get there very early, bring a newspaper or magazine to take your mind off yourself while waiting.
- Locate the examination room – When you have found the proper room, you will be directed to the seat or part of the room where you will sit. Sometimes you are given a sheet of instructions to read while you are waiting. Do not fill out any forms until you are told to do so; just read them and be prepared.
- Relax and prepare to listen to the instructions
- If you have any physical problem that may keep you from doing your best, be sure to tell the test administrator. If you are sick or in poor health, you really cannot do your best on the exam. You can come back and take the test some other time.

VII. AT THE TEST

The day of the test is here and you have the test booklet in your hand. The temptation to get going is very strong. Caution! There is more to success than knowing the right answers. You must know how to identify your papers and understand variations in the type of short-answer question used in this particular examination. Follow these suggestions for maximum results from your efforts:

1) Cooperate with the monitor

The test administrator has a duty to create a situation in which you can be as much at ease as possible. He will give instructions, tell you when to begin, check to see that you are marking your answer sheet correctly, and so on. He is not there to guard you, although he will see that your competitors do not take unfair advantage. He wants to help you do your best.

2) Listen to all instructions

Don't jump the gun! Wait until you understand all directions. In most civil service tests you get more time than you need to answer the questions. So don't be in a hurry. Read each word of instructions until you clearly understand the meaning. Study the examples, listen to all announcements and follow directions. Ask questions if you do not understand what to do.

3) Identify your papers

Civil service exams are usually identified by number only. You will be assigned a number; you must not put your name on your test papers. Be sure to copy your number correctly. Since more than one exam may be given, copy your exact examination title.

4) Plan your time

Unless you are told that a test is a "speed" or "rate of work" test, speed itself is usually not important. Time enough to answer all the questions will be provided, but this does not mean that you have all day. An overall time limit has been set. Divide the total time (in minutes) by the number of questions to determine the approximate time you have for each question.

5) Do not linger over difficult questions

If you come across a difficult question, mark it with a paper clip (useful to have along) and come back to it when you have been through the booklet. One caution if you do this – be sure to skip a number on your answer sheet as well. Check often to be sure that you have not lost your place and that you are marking in the row numbered the same as the question you are answering.

6) Read the questions

Be sure you know what the question asks! Many capable people are unsuccessful because they failed to *read* the questions correctly.

7) Answer all questions

Unless you have been instructed that a penalty will be deducted for incorrect answers, it is better to guess than to omit a question.

8) Speed tests

It is often better NOT to guess on speed tests. It has been found that on timed tests people are tempted to spend the last few seconds before time is called in marking answers at random – without even reading them – in the hope of picking up a few extra points. To discourage this practice, the instructions may warn you that your score will be "corrected" for guessing. That is, a penalty will be applied. The incorrect answers will be deducted from the correct ones, or some other penalty formula will be used.

9) Review your answers

If you finish before time is called, go back to the questions you guessed or omitted to give them further thought. Review other answers if you have time.

10) Return your test materials

If you are ready to leave before others have finished or time is called, take ALL your materials to the monitor and leave quietly. Never take any test material with you. The monitor can discover whose papers are not complete, and taking a test booklet may be grounds for disqualification.

VIII. EXAMINATION TECHNIQUES

1) Read the general instructions carefully. These are usually printed on the first page of the exam booklet. As a rule, these instructions refer to the timing of the examination; the fact that you should not start work until the signal and must stop work at a signal, etc. If there are any *special* instructions, such as a choice of questions to be answered, make sure that you note this instruction carefully.

2) When you are ready to start work on the examination, that is as soon as the signal has been given, read the instructions to each question booklet, underline any key words or phrases, such as *least, best, outline, describe* and the like. In this way you will tend to answer as requested rather than discover on reviewing your paper that you *listed without describing*, that you selected the *worst* choice rather than the *best* choice, etc.

3) If the examination is of the objective or multiple-choice type – that is, each question will also give a series of possible answers: A, B, C or D, and you are called upon to select the best answer and write the letter next to that answer on your answer paper – it is advisable to start answering each question in turn. There may be anywhere from 50 to 100 such questions in the three or four hours allotted and you can see how much time would be taken if you read through all the questions before beginning to answer any. Furthermore, if you come across a question or group of questions which you know would be difficult to answer, it would undoubtedly affect your handling of all the other questions.

4) If the examination is of the essay type and contains but a few questions, it is a moot point as to whether you should read all the questions before starting to answer any one. Of course, if you are given a choice – say five out of seven and the like – then it is essential to read all the questions so you can eliminate the two that are most difficult. If, however, you are asked to answer all the questions, there may be danger in trying to answer the easiest one first because you may find that you will spend too much time on it. The best technique is to answer the first question, then proceed to the second, etc.

5) Time your answers. Before the exam begins, write down the time it started, then add the time allowed for the examination and write down the time it must be completed, then divide the time available somewhat as follows:

- If 3-1/2 hours are allowed, that would be 210 minutes. If you have 80 objective-type questions, that would be an average of 2-1/2 minutes per question. Allow yourself no more than 2 minutes per question, or a total of 160 minutes, which will permit about 50 minutes to review.
- If for the time allotment of 210 minutes there are 7 essay questions to answer, that would average about 30 minutes a question. Give yourself only 25 minutes per question so that you have about 35 minutes to review.

6) The most important instruction is to *read each question* and make sure you know what is wanted. The second most important instruction is to *time yourself properly* so that you answer every question. The third most important instruction is to *answer every question*. Guess if you have to but include something for each question. Remember that you will receive no credit for a blank and will probably receive some credit if you write something in answer to an essay question. If you guess a letter – say "B" for a multiple-choice question – you may have guessed right. If you leave a blank as an answer to a multiple-choice question, the examiners may respect your feelings but it will not add a point to your score. Some exams may penalize you for wrong answers, so in such cases *only*, you may not want to guess unless you have some basis for your answer.

7) Suggestions
   a. Objective-type questions
      1. Examine the question booklet for proper sequence of pages and questions
      2. Read all instructions carefully
      3. Skip any question which seems too difficult; return to it after all other questions have been answered
      4. Apportion your time properly; do not spend too much time on any single question or group of questions
      5. Note and underline key words – *all, most, fewest, least, best, worst, same, opposite,* etc.
      6. Pay particular attention to negatives
      7. Note unusual option, e.g., unduly long, short, complex, different or similar in content to the body of the question
      8. Observe the use of "hedging" words – *probably, may, most likely,* etc.
      9. Make sure that your answer is put next to the same number as the question
      10. Do not second-guess unless you have good reason to believe the second answer is definitely more correct
      11. Cross out original answer if you decide another answer is more accurate; do not erase until you are ready to hand your paper in
      12. Answer all questions; guess unless instructed otherwise
      13. Leave time for review

   b. Essay questions
      1. Read each question carefully
      2. Determine exactly what is wanted. Underline key words or phrases.
      3. Decide on outline or paragraph answer

4. Include many different points and elements unless asked to develop any one or two points or elements
5. Show impartiality by giving pros and cons unless directed to select one side only
6. Make and write down any assumptions you find necessary to answer the questions
7. Watch your English, grammar, punctuation and choice of words
8. Time your answers; don't crowd material

8) Answering the essay question

Most essay questions can be answered by framing the specific response around several key words or ideas. Here are a few such key words or ideas:

M's: manpower, materials, methods, money, management
P's: purpose, program, policy, plan, procedure, practice, problems, pitfalls, personnel, public relations

   a. Six basic steps in handling problems:
1. Preliminary plan and background development
2. Collect information, data and facts
3. Analyze and interpret information, data and facts
4. Analyze and develop solutions as well as make recommendations
5. Prepare report and sell recommendations
6. Install recommendations and follow up effectiveness

   b. Pitfalls to avoid
1. *Taking things for granted* – A statement of the situation does not necessarily imply that each of the elements is necessarily true; for example, a complaint may be invalid and biased so that all that can be taken for granted is that a complaint has been registered
2. *Considering only one side of a situation* – Wherever possible, indicate several alternatives and then point out the reasons you selected the best one
3. *Failing to indicate follow up* – Whenever your answer indicates action on your part, make certain that you will take proper follow-up action to see how successful your recommendations, procedures or actions turn out to be
4. *Taking too long in answering any single question* – Remember to time your answers properly

IX. AFTER THE TEST

Scoring procedures differ in detail among civil service jurisdictions although the general principles are the same. Whether the papers are hand-scored or graded by machine we have described, they are nearly always graded by number. That is, the person who marks the paper knows only the number – never the name – of the applicant. Not until all the papers have been graded will they be matched with names. If other tests, such as training and experience or oral interview ratings have been given, scores will be combined. Different parts of the examination usually have different weights. For example, the written test might count 60 percent of the final grade, and a rating of training and experience 40 percent. In many jurisdictions, veterans will have a certain number of points added to their grades.

After the final grade has been determined, the names are placed in grade order and an eligible list is established. There are various methods for resolving ties between those who get the same final grade – probably the most common is to place first the name of the person whose application was received first. Job offers are made from the eligible list in the order the names appear on it. You will be notified of your grade and your rank as soon as all these computations have been made. This will be done as rapidly as possible.

People who are found to meet the requirements in the announcement are called "eligibles." Their names are put on a list of eligible candidates. An eligible's chances of getting a job depend on how high he stands on this list and how fast agencies are filling jobs from the list.

When a job is to be filled from a list of eligibles, the agency asks for the names of people on the list of eligibles for that job. When the civil service commission receives this request, it sends to the agency the names of the three people highest on this list. Or, if the job to be filled has specialized requirements, the office sends the agency the names of the top three persons who meet these requirements from the general list.

The appointing officer makes a choice from among the three people whose names were sent to him. If the selected person accepts the appointment, the names of the others are put back on the list to be considered for future openings.

That is the rule in hiring from all kinds of eligible lists, whether they are for typist, carpenter, chemist, or something else. For every vacancy, the appointing officer has his choice of any one of the top three eligibles on the list. This explains why the person whose name is on top of the list sometimes does not get an appointment when some of the persons lower on the list do. If the appointing officer chooses the second or third eligible, the No. 1 eligible does not get a job at once, but stays on the list until he is appointed or the list is terminated.

X. HOW TO PASS THE INTERVIEW TEST

The examination for which you applied requires an oral interview test. You have already taken the written test and you are now being called for the interview test – the final part of the formal examination.

You may think that it is not possible to prepare for an interview test and that there are no procedures to follow during an interview. Our purpose is to point out some things you can do in advance that will help you and some good rules to follow and pitfalls to avoid while you are being interviewed.

What is an interview supposed to test?

The written examination is designed to test the technical knowledge and competence of the candidate; the oral is designed to evaluate intangible qualities, not readily measured otherwise, and to establish a list showing the relative fitness of each candidate – as measured against his competitors – for the position sought. Scoring is not on the basis of "right" and "wrong," but on a sliding scale of values ranging from "not passable" to "outstanding." As a matter of fact, it is possible to achieve a relatively low score without a single "incorrect" answer because of evident weakness in the qualities being measured.

Occasionally, an examination may consist entirely of an oral test – either an individual or a group oral. In such cases, information is sought concerning the technical knowledges and abilities of the candidate, since there has been no written examination for this purpose. More commonly, however, an oral test is used to supplement a written examination.

Who conducts interviews?

The composition of oral boards varies among different jurisdictions. In nearly all, a representative of the personnel department serves as chairman. One of the members of the board may be a representative of the department in which the candidate would work. In some cases, "outside experts" are used, and, frequently, a businessman or some other representative of the general public is asked to serve. Labor and management or other special groups may be represented. The aim is to secure the services of experts in the appropriate field.

However the board is composed, it is a good idea (and not at all improper or unethical) to ascertain in advance of the interview who the members are and what groups they represent. When you are introduced to them, you will have some idea of their backgrounds and interests, and at least you will not stutter and stammer over their names.

What should be done before the interview?

While knowledge about the board members is useful and takes some of the surprise element out of the interview, there is other preparation which is more substantive. It *is* possible to prepare for an oral interview – in several ways:

1) Keep a copy of your application and review it carefully before the interview

This may be the only document before the oral board, and the starting point of the interview. Know what education and experience you have listed there, and the sequence and dates of all of it. Sometimes the board will ask you to review the highlights of your experience for them; you should not have to hem and haw doing it.

2) Study the class specification and the examination announcement

Usually, the oral board has one or both of these to guide them. The qualities, characteristics or knowledges required by the position sought are stated in these documents. They offer valuable clues as to the nature of the oral interview. For example, if the job involves supervisory responsibilities, the announcement will usually indicate that knowledge of modern supervisory methods and the qualifications of the candidate as a supervisor will be tested. If so, you can expect such questions, frequently in the form of a hypothetical situation which you are expected to solve. NEVER go into an oral without knowledge of the duties and responsibilities of the job you seek.

3) Think through each qualification required

Try to visualize the kind of questions you would ask if you were a board member. How well could you answer them? Try especially to appraise your own knowledge and background in each area, *measured against the job sought*, and identify any areas in which you are weak. Be critical and realistic – do not flatter yourself.

4) Do some general reading in areas in which you feel you may be weak

For example, if the job involves supervision and your past experience has NOT, some general reading in supervisory methods and practices, particularly in the field of human relations, might be useful. Do NOT study agency procedures or detailed manuals. The oral board will be testing your understanding and capacity, not your memory.

5) Get a good night's sleep and watch your general health and mental attitude

You will want a clear head at the interview. Take care of a cold or any other minor ailment, and of course, no hangovers.

What should be done on the day of the interview?

Now comes the day of the interview itself. Give yourself plenty of time to get there. Plan to arrive somewhat ahead of the scheduled time, particularly if your appointment is in the fore part of the day. If a previous candidate fails to appear, the board might be ready for you a bit early. By early afternoon an oral board is almost invariably behind schedule if there are many candidates, and you may have to wait. Take along a book or magazine to read, or your application to review, but leave any extraneous material in the waiting room when you go in for your interview. In any event, relax and compose yourself.

The matter of dress is important. The board is forming impressions about you – from your experience, your manners, your attitude, and your appearance. Give your personal appearance careful attention. Dress your best, but not your flashiest. Choose conservative, appropriate clothing, and be sure it is immaculate. This is a business interview, and your appearance should indicate that you regard it as such. Besides, being well groomed and properly dressed will help boost your confidence.

Sooner or later, someone will call your name and escort you into the interview room. *This is it.* From here on you are on your own. It is too late for any more preparation. But remember, you asked for this opportunity to prove your fitness, and you are here because your request was granted.

What happens when you go in?

The usual sequence of events will be as follows: The clerk (who is often the board stenographer) will introduce you to the chairman of the oral board, who will introduce you to the other members of the board. Acknowledge the introductions before you sit down. Do not be surprised if you find a microphone facing you or a stenotypist sitting by. Oral interviews are usually recorded in the event of an appeal or other review.

Usually the chairman of the board will open the interview by reviewing the highlights of your education and work experience from your application – primarily for the benefit of the other members of the board, as well as to get the material into the record. Do not interrupt or comment unless there is an error or significant misinterpretation; if that is the case, do not hesitate. But do not quibble about insignificant matters. Also, he will usually ask you some question about your education, experience or your present job – partly to get you to start talking and to establish the interviewing "rapport." He may start the actual questioning, or turn it over to one of the other members. Frequently, each member undertakes the questioning on a particular area, one in which he is perhaps most competent, so you can expect each member to participate in the examination. Because time is limited, you may also expect some rather abrupt switches in the direction the questioning takes, so do not be upset by it. Normally, a board member will not pursue a single line of questioning unless he discovers a particular strength or weakness.

After each member has participated, the chairman will usually ask whether any member has any further questions, then will ask you if you have anything you wish to add. Unless you are expecting this question, it may floor you. Worse, it may start you off on an extended, extemporaneous speech. The board is not usually seeking more information. The question is principally to offer you a last opportunity to present further qualifications or to indicate that you have nothing to add. So, if you feel that a significant qualification or characteristic has been overlooked, it is proper to point it out in a sentence or so. Do not compliment the board on the thoroughness of their examination – they have been sketchy, and you know it. If you wish, merely say, "No thank you, I have nothing further to add." This is a point where you can "talk yourself out" of a good impression or fail to present an important bit of information. Remember, *you close the interview yourself.*

The chairman will then say, "That is all, Mr. _____, thank you." Do not be startled; the interview is over, and quicker than you think. Thank him, gather your belongings and take your leave. Save your sigh of relief for the other side of the door.

How to put your best foot forward

Throughout this entire process, you may feel that the board individually and collectively is trying to pierce your defenses, seek out your hidden weaknesses and embarrass and confuse you. Actually, this is not true. They are obliged to make an appraisal of your qualifications for the job you are seeking, and they want to see you in your best light. Remember, they must interview all candidates and a non-cooperative candidate may become a failure in spite of their best efforts to bring out his qualifications. Here are 15 suggestions that will help you:

1) Be natural – Keep your attitude confident, not cocky

If you are not confident that you can do the job, do not expect the board to be. Do not apologize for your weaknesses, try to bring out your strong points. The board is interested in a positive, not negative, presentation. Cockiness will antagonize any board member and make him wonder if you are covering up a weakness by a false show of strength.

2) Get comfortable, but don't lounge or sprawl

Sit erectly but not stiffly. A careless posture may lead the board to conclude that you are careless in other things, or at least that you are not impressed by the importance of the occasion. Either conclusion is natural, even if incorrect. Do not fuss with your clothing, a pencil or an ashtray. Your hands may occasionally be useful to emphasize a point; do not let them become a point of distraction.

3) Do not wisecrack or make small talk

This is a serious situation, and your attitude should show that you consider it as such. Further, the time of the board is limited – they do not want to waste it, and neither should you.

4) Do not exaggerate your experience or abilities

In the first place, from information in the application or other interviews and sources, the board may know more about you than you think. Secondly, you probably will not get away with it. An experienced board is rather adept at spotting such a situation, so do not take the chance.

5) If you know a board member, do not make a point of it, yet do not hide it
Certainly you are not fooling him, and probably not the other members of the board. Do not try to take advantage of your acquaintanceship – it will probably do you little good.

6) Do not dominate the interview
Let the board do that. They will give you the clues – do not assume that you have to do all the talking. Realize that the board has a number of questions to ask you, and do not try to take up all the interview time by showing off your extensive knowledge of the answer to the first one.

7) Be attentive
You only have 20 minutes or so, and you should keep your attention at its sharpest throughout. When a member is addressing a problem or question to you, give him your undivided attention. Address your reply principally to him, but do not exclude the other board members.

8) Do not interrupt
A board member may be stating a problem for you to analyze. He will ask you a question when the time comes. Let him state the problem, and wait for the question.

9) Make sure you understand the question
Do not try to answer until you are sure what the question is. If it is not clear, restate it in your own words or ask the board member to clarify it for you. However, do not haggle about minor elements.

10) Reply promptly but not hastily
A common entry on oral board rating sheets is "candidate responded readily," or "candidate hesitated in replies." Respond as promptly and quickly as you can, but do not jump to a hasty, ill-considered answer.

11) Do not be peremptory in your answers
A brief answer is proper – but do not fire your answer back. That is a losing game from your point of view. The board member can probably ask questions much faster than you can answer them.

12) Do not try to create the answer you think the board member wants
He is interested in what kind of mind you have and how it works – not in playing games. Furthermore, he can usually spot this practice and will actually grade you down on it.

13) Do not switch sides in your reply merely to agree with a board member
Frequently, a member will take a contrary position merely to draw you out and to see if you are willing and able to defend your point of view. Do not start a debate, yet do not surrender a good position. If a position is worth taking, it is worth defending.

14) Do not be afraid to admit an error in judgment if you are shown to be wrong

The board knows that you are forced to reply without any opportunity for careful consideration. Your answer may be demonstrably wrong. If so, admit it and get on with the interview.

15) Do not dwell at length on your present job

The opening question may relate to your present assignment. Answer the question but do not go into an extended discussion. You are being examined for a *new* job, not your present one. As a matter of fact, try to phrase ALL your answers in terms of the job for which you are being examined.

Basis of Rating

Probably you will forget most of these "do's" and "don'ts" when you walk into the oral interview room. Even remembering them all will not ensure you a passing grade. Perhaps you did not have the qualifications in the first place. But remembering them will help you to put your best foot forward, without treading on the toes of the board members.

Rumor and popular opinion to the contrary notwithstanding, an oral board wants you to make the best appearance possible. They know you are under pressure – but they also want to see how you respond to it as a guide to what your reaction would be under the pressures of the job you seek. They will be influenced by the degree of poise you display, the personal traits you show and the manner in which you respond.

ABOUT THIS BOOK

This book contains tests divided into Examination Sections. Go through each test, answering every question in the margin. At the end of each test look at the answer key and check your answers. On the ones you got wrong, look at the right answer choice and learn. Do not fill in the answers first. Do not memorize the questions and answers, but understand the answer and principles involved. On your test, the questions will likely be different from the samples. Questions are changed and new ones added. If you understand these past questions you should have success with any changes that arise. Tests may consist of several types of questions. We have additional books on each subject should more study be advisable or necessary for you. Finally, the more you study, the better prepared you will be. This book is intended to be the last thing you study before you walk into the examination room. Prior study of relevant texts is also recommended. NLC publishes some of these in our Fundamental Series. Knowledge and good sense are important factors in passing your exam. Good luck also helps. So now study this Passbook, absorb the material contained within and take that knowledge into the examination. Then do your best to pass that exam.

www.ingramcontent.com/pod-product-compliance
Lightning Source LLC
Chambersburg PA
CBHW080516110426
42742CB00017B/3136